THE MANUSCRIPT OF SHAKESPEARE'S *HAMLET* AND THE PROBLEMS OF ITS TRANSMISSION

IN TWO VOLUMES

VOLUME I

THE MANUSCRIPT OF SHAKESPEARE'S *HAMLET* AND THE PROBLEMS OF ITS TRANSMISSION

An essay in critical bibliography

BY

J. DOVER WILSON, Litt.D., F.B.A.

SANDARS READER IN BIBLIOGRAPHY
1932

VOLUME I

THE TEXTS OF 1605 AND 1623

CAMBRIDGE
AT THE UNIVERSITY PRESS
1963

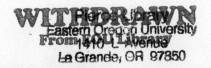

PUBLISHED BY
THE SYNDICS OF THE CAMBRIDGE UNIVERSITY PRESS

Bentley House, 200 Euston Road, London, N.W. 1
American Branch: 32 East 57th Street, New York 22, N.Y.
West African Office: P.O. Box 33, Ibadan, Nigeria

First printed 1934
Reprinted 1963

First printed in Great Britain at the University Press, Cambridge
Reprinted by offset-litho by
Billing and Sons Limited, Guildford and London

TO
A.W.P.
Sandars Reader
1915

CONTENTS

VOL. I. THE TEXTS OF 1605 AND 1623

VOL. II. EDITORIAL PROBLEMS AND SOLUTIONS

FOREWORD
TO THE 1963 IMPRESSION

Though subsequent developments in Shakespearian textual study have rendered these volumes to some extent out of date, there are good reasons why they should be reissued now. For one thing, there is much in them that remains valid; and for another thing, they constitute a landmark in the evolution of a particular kind of scholarship which has its own historical interest.

Along with Pollard, Greg, McKerrow, and others, with whom in their times he was closely associated, Professor Dover Wilson is often said to belong to the "bibliographical school" of Shakespearian textual students. McKerrow took exception to the use of the term. "It is, I think, very unfortunate," he writes,[1] "that attempts to determine the causes of the condition of the [early Shakespearian] texts seem to have come to be called by the general name of 'bibliographical' study of these texts. The only reason for the name seems to be that some of the principal scholars who have interested themselves in such research, such as Dr A. W. Pollard and Dr W. W. Greg, have *also* been bibliographers. There is nothing particularly 'bibliographical' about most of the arguments used." Certainly much in the textual work of this group lies outside the field of bibliography properly so called; but, *pace* McKerrow, much of it lies within that field, and the present monograph is quite rightly sub-titled "An essay in critical bibliography".

Though there had earlier been tentative and partial

---

[1] *Prolegomena for the Oxford Shakespeare*, 1939, p. 9, note 2.

application of bibliographical methods to Shakespearian textual study (notably in the work of P. A. Daniel), it was not until the beginning of this century that the movement really got under way. Pollard's *Shakespeare Folios and Quartos* appeared in 1909 "at a moment", according to Greg,[1] "when the connexion between bibliographical and literary investigation was first attracting wider attention". From then on, bibliographical and partly bibliographical contributions to the study of Shakespeare's text came thick and fast, from many hands. The history of "Shakespeare and the 'New Bibliography'" up to the middle of 1942 has been traced by Professor F. P. Wilson in an elaborate article[2] of great value.

It is not a romantic irrelevance to recall that in the early decades of the century the development of the new Shakespearian textual scholarship proceeded in an atmosphere of considerable excitement. Researchers were often conscious of setting their feet on hazardous paths. Sometimes they took wrong turnings, and the right road had to be rediscovered. Sometimes a highly ingenious theory was proposed and then abandoned by its own originator. Much work was experimental, and the results were often advanced as tentative and provisional. Some scholars were more cautious and guarded than others: some were more daring and speculative, more enterprising and adventurous, than others. Professor Dover Wilson has said in one of his most recent volumes[3] that the editing of Shakespeare is "an endless adventure". His own work, textual as well as literary, has always had this adventurous quality, and indeed he is sometimes criticised for carrying it to excess. But,

---

[1] *The Bibliographical Society, 1892–1942. Studies in Retrospect,* 1945, p. 29.

[2] *Ibid.* pp. 76–135.

[3] *The New Shakespeare,* "King Lear", 1960, p. viii.

while this criticism may legitimately be made at this or that point in the corpus of his writings, more must be said in order to give a balanced estimate. *The Manuscript of Shakespeare's "Hamlet"* (or *MSH* for short) gives ample proof of his willingness and ability to undertake careful, methodical, and laborious spade-work which will for long be indispensable to other scholars in the field. In an important book of recent date, Dr Alice Walker, while dissenting from certain of Dover Wilson's views on the text of *Hamlet*, points out how useful it is to have a classi-fication of the variants, and an interpretation of them which later scholars can accept, or modify and supplement.[1]

Still useful now, *MSH* nevertheless belongs to a pioneering epoch, and the study of bibliography in relation to textual criticism has made remarkable advances since 1934. Much of the latest work has been, and is being, done by American scholars. Prominent among these are Dr Fredson Bowers and Dr Charlton Hinman, though numerous others should also be mentioned; and in this country Dr Walker's is the outstanding (though again not the only) name. Special mention should be made of her book *Textual Problems of the First Folio* (1953), which has achieved widespread recognition as (in Greg's words)[2] "the most penetrating contribution to the study of Shake-speare's text that has appeared for a considerable time".

Bibliography is studied by these latest textual scholars in greater detail, and with more scientific precision, than by textual scholars heretofore. Nowadays the editor of a Shakespeare play must be prepared to undergo a more rigorous and far-reaching technical training than his pre-decessors had; otherwise he risks adverse criticism of the kind bestowed by Dr Bowers on some of the textual work

[1] *Textual Problems of the First Folio*, 1953, p. 121.
[2] *The Editorial Problem in Shakespeare*, 3rd edition, 1954, Preface.

in *The New Shakespeare*. It may be that some of us stand a little more in awe of the Virginia school[1] of bibliographers than is absolutely necessary. Time will tell. But at any rate it must be allowed that much more is known now about the actual printing of the early Shakespeare texts than was known in 1934. Moreover, the editorial methods advocated by the specialists of whom I am speaking are more strictly controlled by specifically bibliographical considerations than is the case in some of the volumes of *The New Shakespeare*. *MSH* is based on the Sandars lectures given in the University of Cambridge in 1932. In 1959 Dr Bowers published his *Textual and Literary Criticism*, the greater part of which is essentially the Sandars lectures given in 1958. If the reader will look at the third of Dr Bowers's chapters, "The New Textual Criticism of Shakespeare", he will see the direction in which bibliographical techniques in textual study have moved since Dover Wilson's monograph on *Hamlet* appeared. Reference should also be made to Bowers's *On Editing Shakespeare and the Elizabethan Dramatists* (1955), which gives the text of the Rosenbach lectures which he delivered in the University of Pennsylvania in 1954.

Of cardinal importance in the latest research is compositor-determination. The work of different compositors is separated out, their individual habits (e.g. of spelling) having been distinguished: the work done by this or that compositor on different plays is scrutinised, and the way in which each dealt with different kinds of copy is studied: their relative proneness to error is established: and so on. Detailed technical investigation often leads to conclusions

---

[1] I hope that this term will not give offence. I use it mainly because much of the work of the latest bibliographical critics is to be found in *Studies in Bibliography*, the Papers of the Bibliographical Society of the University of Virginia, 1948 onwards.

different from those of Dover Wilson. The study of Q2 in *MSH* gives us, as Mr John Russell Brown[1] says, "one of the first attempts to analyse the habits of a compositor in an Elizabethan printing house". But this pioneer bibliographical analysis led to results which, it seems, require modification. In 1934 Dover Wilson thought that Q2 *Hamlet* was set by a single compositor who was an unskilful workman, and who happened to be a Welshman. Mr Brown maintains that it was set by two compositors, X and Y—the same two who collaborated on the 1600 quarto of *The Merchant of Venice*. In the course of the lectures to which I have referred,[2] Dr Bowers (with acknowledgements where they are due) virtually shows us into the printing-house. We see X and Y at work, each setting different sheets, neither of them being inexperienced. We see X working more quickly than Y: we see X giving Y a helping hand at one point: we see Y working in some places more rapidly than his normal. Equipped with such information, an editor is enabled "to make at least some rough equation between the amount of emendation necessary sheet by sheet, depending upon which compositor set it and on the estimate whether it was set at a normal or an abnormal rate of speed". Further, logical use of the scientifically established evidence leads us to infer that "the copy given to the printer was not so illegible or in such general bad shape as has customarily been supposed". Again, Mr Brown's analysis of the two compositors has indicated, Bowers says, "that various spellings in the quarto *Hamlet* that Dover Wilson had isolated as authentically Shakespeare's own are in fact merely compositorial". Compositor-determination is also important, of course, in connection

[1] *Studies in Bibliography*, VII (1955), 17.
[2] *On Editing Shakespeare*, pp. 38–40; *Textual and Literary Criticism*, pp. 77, 111.

with the folio text of the play. F *Hamlet*, it appears, was set by three compositors, *A*, *B*, and *E*, the last-mentioned being an apprentice hand. In dealing with *Hamlet*, the editor of the future will, as Bowers says, "estimate the authority of Folio readings. . . somewhat differently depending upon whether compositor *A*, or *B*, or the apprentice *E* set the type". We cannot simply speak of "the folio *Hamlet*" as having the same degree of authority throughout.

In certain respects Bowers is able to speak of bibliographical techniques as leading to incontrovertible results.[1] On the other hand, the reader must not be given the impression that this critic claims more for bibliography than in fact he does. As regards the editing of Shakespeare, Bowers feels that as yet "we are not properly ready for anything but provisional results";[2] and again, he does not regard bibliography as supplying the only necessary key. Language study is needed, and also "literary criticism shaping the judgement *within certain limits prescribed by bibliography and language*" (the italics are his). Bibliography is not all that is necessary, but it is necessary: and Bowers' principal complaint against Dover Wilson is that the latter is prone to use non-bibliographical methods—that he is, to speak informally, not bibliographical enough. In the twentieth century, Bowers declares, "a *little* bibliography has sometimes become a rather dangerous thing".

The rapid and spectacular advances in bibliographical study since the Second World War must not delude us into a false confidence. The latest bibliographical methods

---

[1] E.g. "Dr Hinman's researches, when fully published in the future, will identify on irrefutable evidence the work of all the Folio compositors, even to the part-column" (*Textual and Literary Criticism*, p. 78).

[2] See *Textual and Literary Criticism*, pp. 69, 116.

have not, for example, brought us certainty about the text of *Hamlet*. It is, I think, generally conceded that Dover Wilson is right in supposing that Q2 was for the most part printed from Shakespeare's foul papers: but there is disagreement regarding the involvement of Q1 in the portion of text we call Act I. Was there occasional Q2 compositorial consultation of Q1 in Act I, as Dover Wilson holds; or was Q2 set throughout Act I from a Q1 edited from the foul papers, and set thereafter from the foul papers themselves, as Dr Walker has more recently maintained?[1] And a more extensive problem is still in dispute—what was the exact nature of the copy for F, and what is the exact relationship between F and Q2? In the present monograph (p. 66) Dover Wilson says "It is clear that the 1605 *Hamlet* or its reprints, the Smethwick quartos, do not at any point come into the pedigree of the F1 text". This cannot now be accepted. We are looking forward to two important new editions of *Hamlet*, that in *The Oxford Shakespeare* (Dr Alice Walker) and that in the new *Arden Shakespeare* (Professor Harold Jenkins). Both of these scholars have published their textual theories of the play, and they differ on the nature of the copy for F. According to Dr Walker,[2] F was printed from an edited copy of Q2, the corrections having been taken from the prompt-book in use in 1621–3, and this prompt-book was itself a transcript of the original prompt-book. According to Professor Jenkins,[3] F was not printed from an edited Q2 but from a transcript of the prompt-book, the scribe having consulted Q2 sporadically. The experts still disagree; but it seems clear enough that to some extent Q2 does underlie F.

This is not the only case in Shakespeare where it is

[1] *Op. cit.* pp. 121–2.
[2] *Ibid.*
[3] *Studies in Bibliography*, VII (1955), 69–83.

difficult to decide whether a later printed text was set (a) from an earlier printed text edited by comparison with a manuscript, or (b) from a manuscript, with occasional consultation of an earlier printed text.[1] It is equally true in both cases, be it noted, that agreement between the two printed texts is no evidence of authenticity. If F *Hamlet* was printed throughout from an edited Q2, then agreement between F and Q2 is no evidence of authenticity, since at any point the collator may have neglected to make a necessary correction in his Q2, and corruption in Q2 need not always be self-evident. Equally, if F *Hamlet* was printed from an independent manuscript but with sporadic scribal or compositorial consultation of Q2, then agreement between F and Q2 is still no evidence of authenticity, since any F reading may have been taken by scribe or compositor from Q2, and, again, corruption in Q2 need not always be self-evident. In the case of theory (b) it would, of course, be of enormous value if we could determine the extent, or the probable extent, of the consultation of the earlier printed text; but, for *Hamlet*, Professor Jenkins has to conclude his article on a somewhat pessimistic note—how much the scribe who prepared the manuscript copy for F consulted Q2 'will not be easy to determine'.

Essentially an extended 'Note on the Copy', *MSH* is virtually a part of *The New Shakespeare*, an edition which is just on the point of completion after more than forty years of devoted labour by Professor Dover Wilson.[2] *The New Shakespeare* has from the start been controversial, but few will deny its importance. One of the most judicious of

---

[1] Of course, different portions of a given printed text may have been set up from different kinds of copy.

[2] Other hands have been involved, most notably that of Quiller-Couch; but Dover Wilson's work is certainly the main element, and gives the edition its unique character.

American scholars, Professor G. Blakemore Evans, has recently paid tribute to edition and editor,[1] in words which are fully justified. He speaks of *The New Shakespeare* as "one of the most significant editorial undertakings of this century"; and he goes on to say that the edition "must be recognized both for its major contributions to Shakespeare scholarship and for the stimulation it has given to a whole generation of students of Shakespeare to attack afresh a host of problems, textual and critical. Professor Wilson deserves the admiration and gratitude of all lovers of Shakespeare, lay and learned". That some of his theories on the text of *Hamlet* must be abandoned or modified does not alter the fact that *MSH* remains an indispensable piece of apparatus for the present-day scholar; and it is highly desirable that it should be once again in print.

G. I. DUTHIE

[1] *Journal of English and Germanic Philology*, April 1961, p. 323.

PREFACE

This study of the text of Shakespeare's *Hamlet*, its transmission, corruption and restoration, is an expansion of four lectures delivered at Cambridge in November 1932 under the terms of the Sandars Readership in Bibliography. It is also part of a general attack upon the problems of that play which, begun in the autumn of 1917 as a diversion from the anxieties of the tensest months of the Great War, is now drawing to a close in the spring of 1934, after what it may be hoped will prove the most trying years of the Peace. The whole enterprise has been carried through in the scanty leisure hours of an otherwise busy man, and it is only during the last few months, owing to the grant of a Leverhulme Fellowship, that he has been able to give an undistracted mind to it. Yet he counts himself more fortunate than most to have had for sixteen years Shakespeare's Elsinore to fly to and its enthralling and inexhaustible problems to ponder, as a refuge from the pressure of his ordinary duties and as a solace for world-hopes constantly deferred.

These two volumes, then, form the first of three books on *Hamlet*, now all under way; the second being an edition of the play in "The New Shakespeare" and the third an attempt to solve some of the dramatic difficulties which have vexed critics for more than a hundred and fifty years. There are, in fact, three groups of *Hamlet* problems: textual, exegetic, and dramatic. They are distinct, and require different instruments for their manipulation. Yet no group can be satisfactorily handled apart from the others. It is impossible, for example, to be certain that we have justly estimated Hamlet's character, until we know the meaning of everything that he says and that other characters say about him, while it is equally impossible to be certain what the speakers say until we have made up our minds exactly what Shakespeare intended to write. The textual problems are therefore fundamental. Yet they cannot be solved in isolation or without regard to exegetic and dramatic considerations. In other words, this book could not have been written, had I not been editing the play at the same time, i.e. attempting to determine the meaning of every sentence in the text; and had I not at the same time also been working out a detailed and coherent explanation, in terms of the Elizabethan theatre, of the action of the play from Barnardo's challenge "Who's there?" to the command of Fortinbras, "Go, bid the soldiers shoot". A single emendation or choice of variants, even at times the position of a comma or semicolon, may involve first-class issues of poetic criticism or dramatic interpretation. Some of my glosses will be wrong; my reading of character and action will perhaps often go astray; certainly there will be much for conservative critics to dispute. But it must, I think, be admitted that the method is right, that it is indeed the only method which has any chance of success with the most baffling of all Shakespeare's plays, although no one has ever tried it before. Thus, though this book can be read independently of those that are to follow, I would ask any who find difficulty in subscribing to particular conclusions, especially in the second volume, to suspend judgment until he has seen what can be said upon the matter from the point of view of the editor and the dramatic critic.

The campaign began sixteen years ago with simultaneous attacks upon the textual and dramatic problems; and so little did I realise what I was doing that in both cases I selected the most difficult points of all for my attempt: the Playscene, on the dramatic side, and the First Quarto, on the textual. The former topic does not here concern us. Upon the latter I published articles during 1918 in Dr Pollard's periodical *The Library*, articles now long out of print and, I trust, out of reach of all but discreet readers; for though I think they made some advance in the right direction, if

I ever find time to take them up again, I shall revise them drastically.[1] I soon found, indeed, that I had been trying to enter by the wrong door, and that if any final solution of the bad quarto could be hoped for we must first make up our minds quite definitely about the character of the two good texts, seeing that in them and in them alone is to be found the bibliographical basis necessary for such a solution. I soon, too, lost interest in the antics of a pirate, as the fascinating character of the larger problems presented by the Second Quarto and the Folio texts grew upon me: the complexity and multiplicity of their detail, the revelation they offer on the one hand of the practices at the Globe and on the other hand of Shakespeare's subtler intentions which the Globe missed, and above all the increasing certainty that in the Second Quarto we possess what may, without undue presumption, be described as a typographical facsimile, however vilely printed, of the autograph manuscript of the greatest play in the world.

I had set out to discover what sort of wild ass had perpetrated the ridiculous text of 1603, and I found myself before the citadel of Shakespeare's kingdom. Even so, I began once more trying to force an entrance with the wrong key—by offering emendations! Fortunately, I was early distracted from this attempt to plunder the granary before the field had been tilled by a suggestion from Dr Pollard, that I should do an honest piece of spade-work and collect the misprints and strange spellings in the good Shakespearian quartos, and by a request from the Syndics of the Cambridge University Press that I should collaborate with Sir Arthur Quiller-Couch in the edition of the complete works of Shakespeare. These tasks meant laying *Hamlet* aside. But only for a time; and as experience of handling all sorts of Shakespearian texts, both for what came to be called "The New Shakespeare" and for a series of Folio

[1] In this connexion I should mention an important book on the subject published by Signor Giovanni Ramello in 1930.

Facsimiles, issued by Messrs Faber and Faber, increased at once my confidence in the bibliographical method and my caution in utilising it, I came to see that the long road was after all the shortest cut to the end which I kept in view throughout, viz. an edition of *Hamlet* in the light of the new criticism, which was itself to be the preface to an aesthetic study of *Hamlet* already begun in 1918.

The first step towards this edition was taken in 1924 when I published in vol. x of *Essays and Studies by Members of the English Association*, collected by Sir Edmund Chambers, a study of *Spellings and Misprints in the Second Quarto*, in which the apparatus criticus was sketched in outline and an attempt made to apply it to certain outstanding textual problems. Four years later Dr W. W. Greg delivered his British Academy Lecture on *Principles of Emendation in Shakespeare*. Largely devoted to *Hamlet*, and when it appeared in print accompanied with lengthy notes full of important matter, this lecture came to my hands in a happy hour when I had been commissioned by Count Harry Kessler to prepare a text of *Hamlet* for an edition de luxe printed at the Cranach Press. I selected, of course, the Second Quarto version and reproduced it in its original spelling and punctuation, allowing myself no alterations save such as I felt convinced were at once required by misprints and could be justified on graphical principles. The justification involved textual notes, and I owe Count Kessler a great debt of gratitude for his readiness to print these together with a long textual introduction. The Cranach *Hamlet* is, I believe, the only attempt made since the beginning of 1605 to give Shakespeare's text to the world "according to the true and perfect Coppie", as the printer of the Second Quarto claims upon his title-page; and the preparation of it was an education of great value to an editor. For it not only proved, as nothing else could have done, that the Second Quarto had its own rights, but offered a text so superior in subtlety and beauty to the text of the

Folio, upon which all previous editions have been based, as to constitute in effect a new and surprising revelation of Shakespeare's genius. Some day I hope to be allowed to re-print this edition at a price which will place it within the reach of ordinary purses.

Convinced as I now was that the Second Quarto was printed direct from Shakespeare's manuscript and that the Folio *Hamlet* was a text of quite inferior quality, I realised nevertheless that until they knew for certain the origin and make-up of Jaggard's copy in 1623 editors could have no security in dealing with the other and better version. It was, for example, disturbing to find Dr Greg, in his British Academy Lecture, assuming almost as a matter of course that readings in the Folio, more attractive than their variants in the Second Quarto, might be explained as corrections and improvements by Shakespeare himself, introduced into the acting version after it had been copied from the original manuscript. When, therefore, I was appointed Sandars Reader in Bibliography at Cambridge for 1932, I took the text of *Hamlet* as the subject of my lectures and made up my mind not only to sift the problem of the Folio to the bottom but also, if possible, to probe the corruption of the Second Quarto more thoroughly than I had been able to do in the Cranach *Hamlet* or the article in *Essays and Studies*. The book that follows contains as I have said the substance of these lectures, rewritten and considerably en-larged. The second volume in particular, entitled "Editorial Problems and Solutions", has been added since the lectures were delivered. The two volumes, indeed, are intended to serve as a Textual Introduction to the edition of the play for "The New Shakespeare" now in the press. In no other way was it possible for an editor to cope with the multifarious problems which crowded upon him from all quarters in dealing with this extraordinary drama. To edit *Hamlet* on the same scale, for example, as that employed for *Love's Labour's Lost* would demand three volumes. It seemed more convenient to lighten the actual edition by dealing with most of the textual problems first in a separate book to which reference could subsequently be made. Even so, it was not possible to cover all the ground usually traversed in the "Note on the Copy". As I have already remarked, the whole question of the provenance of the bad quarto has had to be left in abeyance. And though I shall not hesitate to make use of that text as an instrument, the reader should clearly understand that I am in no way concerned here with the history of the *Hamlet* text in the sixteenth century. My point of departure is the moment, somewhere probably in the late summer of 1601, when Shakespeare handed over the manuscript of the final *Hamlet* to his fellows at the Globe. What happened to the manuscript after that moment is the theme of this book.

My debt to the three founders and leaders of modern bibliography, Dr Pollard, Dr Greg and Dr McKerrow, can scarcely be overstated. The two first have read the book in proof or typescript and, as my footnotes show, I have freely consulted the third. Indeed, without their suggestions, warnings, and open-handed help generally my task would have been impossible. Even now I cannot hope to have escaped all the dangers which beset one who dares to indulge in bibliographical speculation without ever having worked a hand-press; and I must take full responsibility for every statement or assumption made. For this "essay in critical bibliography" is by a very amateur bibliographer, who if he had realised in 1918 how long the path might prove and across what treacherous bogs it might take him, would never have given chase to the *Hamlet* pirate of 1603. Yet, as I turn over these all too numerous pages before marking them with the irrevocable word "Press", I take reassurance from the thought that, however much my bibliographical conjectures may need revision in the light of fuller knowledge and more patient enquiry, such revision is unlikely to affect seriously the main textual conclusions. In other words,

I have hopes that this book may provide some permanent material for the building of a new *Hamlet*, or rather for the re-building of Shakespeare's *Hamlet*, in place of that Globe *Hamlet* which has for three centuries usurped the site.

Two Dutch monographs have preceded this enterprise, Dr H. de Groot's *Hamlet, its Textual History* (Amsterdam, 1923), and Dr B. A. P. van Dam's *The Text of Shakespeare's Hamlet* (Lane, 1924) and though my methods and conclusions differ widely from theirs, I have learnt from them both. A much nearer approximation to my findings will be found in Sir Edmund Chambers' analysis of the texts of *Hamlet* in Chapter IX of his *William Shakespeare*, 1930. I deliberately avoided reading this section of his book until I had finished my own, and I think it may interest some readers, as it certainly does me, to see where we agree and where we part company. On the whole, I am glad to find, the agreement is remarkably close. I note in particular that he anticipates my explanation of the bibliographical links between Q2 and Q1 in Act I.

I am indebted to the Council of the English Association for kind permission to make free use of the article in vol. X of their *Essays and Studies* referred to above, and to the editors of the *Modern Language Review* for similar permission in regard to articles in that periodical. Finally I have to thank Mrs Murrie, better known to Elizabethan scholars as Eleanore Boswell, for compiling the index and Appendix D, for reading the proofs and for checking all references, a long and arduous undertaking in volumes crowded with detail like these. In the course of this checking she discovered a fresh "correction" in Q2, and I suspect that a more careful and objective reading of the six extant copies than I am now capable of would reveal others.

J. D. W.

April 1934

PREFACE
TO THE 1963 IMPRESSION

In 1955 my attention was drawn to the following reference
to this book by Professor Fredson Bowers:

> It is fair, I think, to say that in the history of *Hamlet's* editors
> from Rowe to Sisson only one man, Dover Wilson, saw the need
> thoroughly to analyze the documents in which the variant forms
> of the text are preserved and to arrive at a coherent theory about
> their origins and relations, before undertaking to edit that text
> according to principles consistent with an overall hypothesis
> dependent upon this analysis.

I was naturally pleased at this unsolicited testimonial from
so eminent a textual critic; but surprised too, since a
Shakespearian editor committed to the complete works and
pushing forward from play to play during the scanty
leisure in an otherwise busy life cannot pay much attention
to other editors and had imagined the book in question,
like Shakespeare's war-horse in front rank, to have been
long since o'errun and trampled on by a far from abject
rear.

It is true Professor Bowers lent some colour to this
supposition by continuing:

> It is apparent now that Wilson did not investigate the docu-
> ments with enough rigor to secure all the available evidence, and
> that he seriously misinterpreted in some important respects the
> evidence he did secure.[1]

Yet after all a book published over a quarter of a century ago
might have expected to encounter a more severe handling

[1] *On Editing Shakespeare and the Elizabethan Dramatists*, 1955,
pp. 4–5.

than this. For there have been greater advances I suppose in our knowledge of the text of Shakespeare during this period than ever before. Indeed, I have myself endeavoured to keep pace with them in the various "Notes on the Copy" to be found in successive volumes of The New Shakespeare, the present book being nothing but an unusually detailed example of such a "Note" separately published but published to coincide with the appearance of the 1934 edition of *Hamlet*.

This *Hamlet* text had since gone into a second edition, and that edition has itself been reprinted five times. But *The Manuscript of Shakespeare's Hamlet* has been long out of print though still to some extent in demand if one may judge from the enquiries of correspondents. And I am encouraged to hope, both by Professor Fredson Bowers' words and by the chapter on *Hamlet* in Dr Alice Walker's valuable *Textual Problems of the First Folio* (1953) which was in some sense a review of my book, that it may be worth making accessible again, if only for its historical interest. Were I twenty years younger I might be tempted to undertake a second and revised edition. As it is, I have turned to two friends for whose help I have never appealed in vain hitherto. Thus Professor Ian Duthie, whose *Bad Quarto of Hamlet* (1941), written while still a student at Edinburgh, was the first to show that his professor had failed to "investigate the documents with enough rigor", has supplied an introduction setting the attempt of 1934 against the background of the textual situation of *Hamlet* as seen today; and Mr J. C. Maxwell when asked for notes upon any particularly glaring errors he may have observed on matters of detail or for queries he felt worth raising, was good enough to send me a sheaf of such notes; and these are now to be found printed at the end of the second volume while daggers have been inserted in the reprint at the points concerned. No reader therefore, however untutored, should have an excuse for attaching undue importance to any statement or conjecture made by an amateur bibliographer in 1934. Let me add, however, that Mr Maxwell warns me that he gives no guarantee that the points he makes are either exhaustive or have not already been made by others.

J. D. W

VOLUME I

THE TEXTS OF 1605 AND 1623

CHAPTER I

Introduction

§ I. THE EDITORIAL TRADITION

What kind of manuscripts lay behind the two main texts of *Hamlet*, that is to say, the quarto edition of 1605 and the folio edition of 1623? What was the relation of these two manuscripts to each other? To what agents are we indebted for their transmission, and how far did these agents influence or modify Shakespeare's original text in the process? Such are the main questions for which we are to attempt to find answers in the first volume of this book. They are the questions of an editor; and the book is written in order that an editor may get on with his work, the next task of which is the preparation of a text of *Hamlet*; a task he will come to grips with in the second volume. The questions come first, however, because until answers are found for them, no satisfactory text of *Hamlet* is possible. Yet though men have been editing *Hamlet* ever since the Second Folio appeared in 1632, three centuries ago, no one has found the answers, and few have even thought it worth while to ask the questions.

We now realise that the steps of most editors of Shakespeare have been dogged by a profound and unwarranted pessimism concerning the texts from which they had to work. "It is impossible to repair the injuries already done him", declared Pope, who was the first to collate the folios with the quartos: "too much time has elapsed, and the materials are too few".[1] Theobald, again, who made even better use of his quartos than Pope, discussing the original

---

[1] Boswell's edition of *Malone's Shakespeare*, 1821, I, 16.

"causes to which the depravations" of Shakespeare's text should be assigned, wrote:

> We are to consider him as a writer, of whom no authentick manuscript was left extant; as a writer, whose pieces were dispersedly performed on the several stages then in being. And it was the custom of those days for the poets to take a price of the players for the pieces they from time to time furnished; and thereupon it was supposed they had no farther right to print them without the consent of the players.... Hence many pieces were taken down in short-hand, and imperfectly copied by ear from a representation; others were printed from piecemeal parts surreptitiously obtained from the theatres, uncorrect, and without the poet's knowledge.[1]

Even Capell, who by no means shared Theobald's views concerning the causes of the "depravations", who made larger claims for the quartos than any previous editor or than most subsequent ones, who actually anticipated Dr Pollard in his distinction between good and bad quartos[2] and in his belief that many of the former may well have been printed from Shakespeare's autographs,[3] confesses that his preference for one text over another and his selection, now from this text and again from that, of "whatever improves the author, or contributes to his advancement in perfectness", were based upon a mere "presumption of genuineness", since the causes of such passages "appearing in some copies, and being wanting in others, cannot now be discover'd, by reason of the time's distance, and defect of fit materials for making the discovery"[4]—words which significantly echo those of Pope just quoted.

Editors in this frame of mind were not likely to take a very profound view of their duties. "The science of

---

[1] Boswell's *Malone's Shakespeare*, I, 32–3.

[2] *Ibid.* pp. 121–2.

[3] *Ibid.* pp. 126–7. Did space allow, I should like to quote at length these remarkable paragraphs, which have been strangely neglected by subsequent critics and display in many ways an astonishingly modern point of view.　　　[4] *Ibid.* pp. 134–5.

criticism, as far as it affects an editor," we read again in Theobald's preface, "seems to be reduced to these three classes: the emendation of corrupt passages; the explanation of obscure and difficult ones; and an enquiry into the beauties and defects of composition."[1] As all the world knows, Theobald took the first of these tasks seriously enough, and scored some signal triumphs in that field; but it is to be noticed that it was as an aid to emendation (by which he meant improving the texts of Rowe and Pope), and for no other purpose, that he turned to the original texts: "As there are very few pages in Shakespeare, upon which some suspicions of depravity do not reasonably arise; I have thought it my duty in the first place, by a diligent and laborious collation, to take in the assistance of all the older copies".[2] There you have an early expression of the editorial ideal of complete textual collation, and of the aims thereof, an ideal which still dominates editorial work, and found its most enduring and magnificent embodiment in *The Cambridge Shakespeare* of 1863–6.

Theobald's words reveal clearly enough the fundamental weakness of this method. The editor starts with a something thoroughly "depraved" which he calls "Shakespeare", and he then proceeds to pour readings from "the older copies" and emendations of his own into this something in order to improve it. And if we enquire what this something actually was, we discover it to be a kind of stock, like that from which cooks make successive potations of soup; for Rowe had based his text upon the Fourth Folio, the last and worst of that series of reprints, Pope based his upon Rowe's, Theobald his upon Pope's, Warburton his upon Theobald's, and Johnson his upon Warburton's. The quality of the original stock improved of course as the "older copies" came to be drawn upon more and more; and Johnson's recognition of the textual supremacy of the First Folio over all other folios was a real turning-point in

[1] Boswell's *Malone's Shakespeare*, I, 34.   [2] *Ibid.* p. 35.

the history of Shakespearian criticism. But the process of concoction remained the same; and though Capell made larger draughts upon the quartos than any previous editor, he continued to collate and to choose his readings according to his own judgment, which was an erratic one, while Jennens, who went even further than Capell in his fidelity to *Hamlet* Q2, found it impossible to remain consistently loyal.

The earliest editor to catch a glimpse of an editor's primary function was Edmond Malone. No other commentator has done more to throw light upon Shakespeare's meaning; yet, as he truly observed, "though to explain and illustrate the writings of our poet is a principal duty of his editor, to ascertain his genuine text, to fix what is to be explained, is his first and immediate object; and till it be established which of the ancient copies is entitled to preference, we have no criterion by which the text can be ascertained".[1] This is admirable; and had editorial theory and practice only followed along the path thus opened up, all might have been well: for the larger outlook which escaped Malone's immediate vision would perhaps have been revealed to his successors. To discover that it was no use beginning to edit before you know what text you have to edit was a great step forward. And yet the next step was never taken.

The reason was, I think, that Malone's statement, sound enough as far as it went, greatly over-simplified the problem at issue. For let us suppose an editor presented with absolute alternatives, presented that is to say with two texts, one of which is to be edited and the other set entirely aside; even so, he has to make his choice between them, and before he can do so he must be quite sure that he knows exactly what the alternatives are. Thus his "first and immediate object" will not be the choice itself, but a preliminary investigation and definition of the texts between

[1] Boswell's *Malone's Shakespeare*, I, 202–3.

which he has to choose. The alternatives, however, at any rate in the case of a play like *Hamlet*, are very far from being absolute. The editor can and certainly ought to decide "which of the ancient copies is entitled to preference", but having done so he is not in a position to concentrate upon that to the neglect of the others. The "genuine text" which is the object of his dreams is a text which corresponds as closely as he can make it with what he believes Shakespeare intended to write, and when as in *Hamlet* both the alternatives are patently imperfect, when, that is to say, one or other of them obviously departs from Shakespeare's intentions in almost every third line, there is nothing for it but to draw upon both for the construction of a sound text, and even at times to turn for light to a third text, still more corrupt. In this parlous condition of affairs, careful definition of the copies becomes of the very highest importance. If we are to help ourselves, now from one text and now from another, it is absolutely essential to know what the texts are, or we may go altogether astray. Here then is the principal purpose of this volume: not "to exhibit the genuine text" of *Hamlet*, which means editing it; not even to decide "which of the ancient copies is entitled to preference", though much will be said under both those heads; but to discover, if possible, just what the two main "ancient copies" were, so that when we come to the final choice and the task of editing we may know where we are and what we are handling.

Hamlet is, of course, a peculiarly difficult problem. It is natural that an editor, committed to "The Complete Works", should allocate more or less the same amount of time to each play and grow restive when a text appears to be demanding an undue share. Now *Hamlet* is not merely the longest of the plays, but from the exegetic standpoint far the most exacting, so that, had only one original text survived, its editing would still probably require twice as much time as that of any other play. As it is, with two texts on his hands, and since the discovery of Q1 in 1821 three, texts moreover which present the most puzzling enigmas of any in the canon, an editor may well shirk the minute examination of his materials which his duty lays upon him. The very magnitude of *Hamlet*, as an editorial undertaking, has induced superficial treatment of its textual foundations. Furthermore, the fact that two texts were available, one traditionally accepted as fundamental since it is descended from the First Folio, and the other its superior at very many points even to the most casual reader, made the method of collation appear at once inevitable and more than usually laborious. It is, indeed, no exaggeration to say that editors have been so busy collating the *Hamlet* texts that they have never found time to consider them apart and to compare them together as two wholes. And when they do venture to express their opinions on this point, they tend to expose themselves most nakedly. It is difficult, for instance, to imagine any generalisation more wrong-headed than the note which appears on the first page of Johnson's *Hamlet* 1768: "This Play is printed both in the folio of 1623, and in the quarto of 1637, more correctly than almost any other of the works of Shakespeare". It is significant to observe, too, that the method of collation was applied to *Hamlet* before any other play, since while Rowe was content in general to follow the Fourth Folio for the rest of the canon, in the case of *Hamlet* he frequently found himself compelled to turn for help to a quarto, that of 1676![1]

[1] I am indebted to Dr R. B. McKerrow for this information. It is of course recognised that Rowe occasionally consulted earlier Folios and even at times a quarto in dealing with other plays (cf. Nichol Smith, *Shakespeare in the XVIIIth Century*, pp. 32–3). I may add here that in writing this Introduction, which stands much as it was delivered as a lecture at Cambridge in 1932, I had not had the advantage of hearing or of reading Dr McKerrow's own lecture on *The Treatment of Shakespeare's Text by his Earlier Editors, 1709–68* delivered before the British Academy in April 1933. In the light of his researches, I should now phrase some sentences differently, but I have thought it best to leave the chapter as it originally stood, since as a matter of fact the points of view do not seriously diverge. My argument would, however, have

And editorial opinion since Rowe's day, as it grew more and more conscious of textual complexity and less and less certain where its true allegiance lay, has shifted this way and that, until in the *Globe* edition of *Hamlet* by Aldis Wright and Clark, issued in 1864, and reproduced, with slight variations, in countless class-books and more popular editions since, it seemed to find an equilibrium about midway between the two originals. In other words, the text of *Hamlet* which passes for genuine with modern readers has been arrived at, not by defining both texts, selecting the better, and using the inferior one with discretion born of knowledge, but by compromising between them on no other principle than that furnished by the good taste and judgment of the editor.

A few figures will help to make the position clear. In Appendix E of the second volume will be found a table of *Hamlet* variants which comprises all the differences between the First Folio and Second Quarto [1] texts of any importance, apart from variants in spelling, punctuation, stage-direction, speech-heading and line-division, which are dealt with elsewhere.[2] This list contains over 1300 items, a figure which is sufficient proof of the seriousness of the textual problem. And when the *Globe Hamlet* is itself considered in the light of the list, we get a striking revelation of the composite character of that text, seeing that it follows F1 in some 630 readings and Q2 in some 540, while it departs from both in 35 instances important enough to be classed as emendations, to say nothing of minor changes which we may for the moment neglect. Let no one suppose, however, that the large number of readings from Q2 indicate any

gained much had I been able to make use of his illuminating observation that in their strange attitude towards the text of Shakespeare, eighteenth and nineteenth century editors were led astray by principles of textual criticism applicable to classical texts (*vide* pp. 20–1 of his lecture).

[1] I shall in future refer to these as F1 and Q2 respectively.
[2] *Vide* Appendix D and vol. II, pp. 182–229.

particular faith in that text. On the contrary, examination shows that the *Globe* editors treated the F1 text, or rather the traditional *Hamlet* derived from it, as the real basis of their edition, since they tend to follow it in stage-directions, assignment of speeches, punctuation and a number of other matters. Moreover, when the 540 readings adopted from Q2 are reviewed they are found to consist for the most part of words or phrases required to fill gaps left in the F1 text by inadvertent omission, of alternative forms such as "my" and "thy" for "mine" and "thine", and of expletives which had been cut out or toned down in the later text in accordance with the statute against blasphemy. When anything serious is at stake, or where the Q2 text presents real difficulty, the editors almost invariably fall back upon F1. In thus leaning upon the text of 1623, they were following tradition, itself misled by the reference to "stolne and surreptitious" quartos in Heminge and Condell's preface, a reference which has only been rightly interpreted by Dr A. W. Pollard within the present generation. But though they lean, they do so with no confidence. They have confidence in neither text; they halt between them, and are unable to make definite choice of either because they are ignorant of the character of both. And if further proof of this be needed, it is furnished by their other edition of *Hamlet*, that published two years later in *The Cambridge Shakespeare*, which differs from its predecessor in 102 readings, 89 of which go in favour of Q2 and 10 in favour of F1.[1] This looks like tardy repentance, until the changes are examined and found to be almost without exception mere trivialities. Nor is any principle evident behind them; they seem nothing but the veerings of a weather-vane.

The unsatisfactory results of this textual vacillation[2] will

---

[1] *The Cambridge Shakespeare* variants are quoted in square brackets beneath those of the *Globe* in the Table of Variants.

[2] That it is possible for a "bibliographical" editor also to vacillate will be evident in §§ XVII and XIX.

be abundantly illustrated in later chapters of this book. Let me, however, quote here a couple of instances by way of enforcing the present argument. At the beginning of act 3, scene 3, Claudius, complaining of Hamlet's behaviour in the Play-scene, declares according to Q2:

> The termes of our estate may not endure
> Hazerd so neer's as doth hourely grow
> Out of his browes

—which is on the face of it absurd; and according to F1:

> The termes of our estate, may not endure
> Hazard so dangerous as doth hourely grow
> Out of his Lunacies

—which on the face of it makes excellent sense. Neither reading, however, finds favour with our collating editors, who combine the two, so that the modern text runs:

> The terms of our estate may not endure
> Hazard so near us as doth hourly grow
> Out of his lunacies.[1]

The train of thought behind this conflation is not difficult to trace. "Browes" is nonsense, "lunacies" is sense; both are found in the "ancient copies"; therefore read "lunacies"—the conclusion seems inevitable. The other variant demands the exercise of judgment and taste; for seeing that "hazard so dangerous" smacks of tautology, to read "hazard so near us" with Q2 is to contribute to that "advancement in perfectness" which Capell sets down as one of the principal aims of an editor of Shakespeare. And so long as editing is nothing more than ladling butter from alternate tubs of unknown manufacture, the combined reading can hardly be improved upon. Yet such a "science of criticism" is strangely unscientific, and its practitioners

---

[1] 3.3.5–7. All references to Shakespeare in this book follow the *Globe* line-numeration; when this differs from that of *Hamlet* in the 'New Shakespeare,' the latter will be found in Appendix E.

curiously incurious.[1] It does not seem to occur to them that two words so different in appearance as "browes" and "lunacies" can hardly both be readings or misreadings of a word which, at whatever remove from the "ancient copies", must once have stood in Shakespeare's original manuscript. They do not ask themselves how such a diversity in the form of the words can have arisen; nor do they enquire whether the readings in the variant pairs, "neer's" and "browes", "dangerous" and "lunacies", may not be textually so closely knit that no editor should put them asunder. In other words, they are not only ignorant of the nature of the copies; they have not even decided which of the two is "entitled to preference".

Nevertheless, such a decision is not enough of itself. For suppose, as we shall discover to be a fact, Q2 turns out to be the better copy of the two, that is to say the nearer to Shakespeare himself, we are not at first sight helped very much thereby with the crux under consideration. True, we shall be encouraged to read "near's", but we shall be left with the nonsense word "browes" on our hands. What are we to do with that? We may decide to emend it. But emendation in our day means something very different from the brilliant shots of a Theobald. Before we can even ask ourselves what word in Shakespeare's manuscript came to be misread "browes", we must know what Shakespearian manuscripts looked like, that is to say, how they were written and how spelt. We must know too what kind of agents of transmission stood between that manuscript and the printed text of Q2, and how these agents were likely to depart from Shakespeare's intentions. In short, in order to emend the single word "browes", an editor must have made an extended study of Shakespeare's ways as a scribe in the texts of other plays and a close study of the idiosyncracies of the Q2 text. Nor is this all. He must further see to it

[1] For Dr McKerrow's explanation of this remarkable attitude, *vide* footnote on p. 7.

that his lines of communication are secure; that is to say, he must explain "lunacies". In other words, he must make up his mind quite definitely on the composition of the F1 text of *Hamlet*, to say nothing at the moment of Q1, if he does not wish to see his whole position, including his emendation of "browes", overthrown, or at any rate attacked from the rear, by some other scholar.

The importance of an exact definition of the two copies becomes even more evident when we turn to the other passage I have selected to illustrate the argument, since here, once again flying in the face of the whole editorial tradition, I believe that F1 should be followed in preference to Q2. "To sing a Requiem" (5. 1. 260) are words given to the churlish priest at Ophelia's funeral by the latter text, words that appear in F1 as "to sing sage Requiem". Now "sage" means grave or dignified, and when Milton in *Il Penseroso* writes

In sage and solemn tunes have sung,

we have an almost exact parallel, which may indeed owe something to the folio *Hamlet*. Rowe, of course, followed F1 here as in most readings, but "sage" seems to have dropped out since; and though Knight and Caldecott tried to revive it early in the nineteenth century, it has failed to win a place in the modern text. The main reason for this remarkable desertion of F1 by editors is, I suspect, sheer ignorance. Despite Milton's use of the word, its meaning had become forgotten and it was taken as printer's nonsense, so that we find, for example, Grant White and Collier attempting to emend it. And yet, once it be rightly interpreted, the temptation to believe it Shakespeare's and to read it in place of the indefinite article of Q2 is very strong indeed, since we feel that no transcriber or compositor can possibly have added it to the text. Nevertheless, we can only read it with confidence if from our knowledge of the texts we can demonstrate one of two things: either (1) that

Shakespeare himself had somehow a finger in the preparation of the F1 version of the play,[1] or (2) that those responsible for the transmission of the Q2 version were prone
first to omit words and then to fill up the metrical lacunae
thus created with makeshift words of their own.[2]

It will, I hope, now be clear that no less wrong-headed
than eclectic editors who pick and choose at their own will,
are those like Jennens who declare almost wholly for Q2
and try to dispense with F1, or those like Delius who swear
fealty to Heminge and Condell and despise the text of 1605.
The simple truth is that no modern text of *Hamlet* is
possible unless both originals are drawn upon, if for no other
reason than because each is full of little omissions which
can only be supplied from the other; and neither Jennens
nor Delius could be consistent in his loyalty. The *Hamlet*
of Delius, however, which appeared in 1854, is interesting
less for itself than for a series of critiques it evoked from
the pen of Tycho Mommsen, wherein a truer and more
penetrating account of the F1 text is rendered than ever
before or since.[3]

In these articles Mommsen demonstrates that the F1
Hamlet displays unmistakable signs of having been deformed
and contaminated by playhouse influences, that it contains
a number of small verbal additions made by the actors, that
it has been moulded throughout to suit the purposes of some
particular theatre, that it gives evidence of careless transcription at many points, and that its metre, line-division
and punctuation have all suffered degradation from the
same cause. Whether the Cambridge editors had read these
articles before they published their own text of 1866 does
not appear. In any event, so wideawake an editor as Aldis

---

[1] Cf. pp. 152–70 below.
[2] Cf. pp. 139–43 below.
[3] *Neue Jahrb. für Phil. und Paed.* Bd. LXXII, 1855, pp. 57–75,
107–27, 159–77. I owe my knowledge of these important articles to
B. A. P. van Dam's *The Text of Shakespeare's Hamlet*, 1924.

Wright could hardly avoid coming to some conclusions on his own account about the nature of the original texts he was handling, and his unqualified statement that "the text of *Hamlet* given in the Folio of 1623 is not derived from any of the previously existing quartos, but from an independent manuscript"[1] must be treated with all the respect due to such an authority. Yet it does not carry us far. And it is not even unambiguous in its meaning. For, as Dr Greg has pointed out, while it might mean that the Q2 and F1 texts were printed from independent manuscripts in the sense that neither was a transcript of the other, it probably implies nothing more than that they were printed from *different* manuscripts.[2]

A later and scarcely less famous editor, Edward Dowden, was either more communicative or more observant, or perhaps he had read Tycho Mommsen. "The Quarto of 1605", he wrote, "is carelessly printed and ill punctuated as compared with *Hamlet* of the Folio, yet it represents more faithfully and fully what Shakespeare wrote. . . . The Folio text was evidently cut for the purpose of stage-representation, and generally it may be described as more theatrical, but less literary, than the text of 1605. . . . Oaths and sacred words are altered to avoid the legal offence of profanity. Some actors' additions are introduced, such as the unhappy 'O, o, o, o' of the dying Hamlet, following his words 'The rest is silence'. And there is a desire evident in the editors of the Folio text to modernise certain words which were regarded as old-fashioned."[3]

This is a real advance on anything previously printed in England on the subject, and though some of the points Dowden makes we shall discover to be erroneous, it is

[1] *The Cambridge Shakespeare*, VII, p. xii.
[2] *Principles of Emendation*, p. 31, note 8. This note appears on p. 156 in *Aspects of Shakespeare*, a volume of British Academy Lectures published by the Clarendon Press in 1933.
[3] *Hamlet* (Arden Shakespeare), Introd. pp. xx–xxi.

doubtful whether he or anyone else could have got further, relying upon general impressions alone. Nevertheless, they remain impressions only, supported by little or no evidence, and certainly uncorroborated by proof; and without proof, or at least probability so strong that it is practically impregnable, all is at hazard; we cannot edit the texts with any sense of security, for at any moment some theorist may arise to challenge our assumptions.

Furthermore, even if we could be certain with Mommsen that a playhouse transcript was handled by the printers in 1623, that would not be sufficient. Before we can use the text critically for emendation and other editorial purposes, before we can even determine its relationship with the Q2 of 1605, we must know more about it. What kind of transcript was it, and by what kind of copyist? To what sort of errors was he prone, and what do they tell us about him and his manuscript? It is enough to anticipate a conclusion we shall reach later, that the manuscript in question, though undoubtedly of playhouse origin, could never have been used for acting in a theatre, to indicate the kind of problems such questions lead on to. Similarly in regard to Q2, it is of little use to an editor to be told that it "is carelessly printed" and yet "represents more faithfully and fully what Shakespeare wrote" than the F1 text. What he wants to know, if he can, is how close it stands to Shakespeare's autograph, and what kind of carelessness its printers were guilty of. In a word, the questions he has to ask are bibliographical questions, and it is just because critical bibliography, which is almost entirely a twentieth-century product, has taught him to ask the right questions that textual criticism and editorial functions have been transformed in our time. Indeed, it was not until 1915 when the leading English bibliographer, Dr A. W. Pollard, delivered the Sandars Lectures of that year at Cambridge, lectures subsequently published as the first volume in the present series under the title of *Shakespeare's Fight with the*

Pirates, that the world became aware of the dawn of a new era in Shakespearian criticism.

Dr Pollard not merely restated the textual problem in scientific terms, he did more; he restored confidence in the "ancient copies". The quartos and the First Folio—especially of course the former—came alive for the first time, and what had seemed to Pope and Theobald and Dr Johnson their irreparable "depravations" were now regarded as bibliographical clues which, if rightly interpreted, might often afford us glimpses of Shakespeare's own manuscripts. This renewal of confidence at once led to a revival of textual criticism, which under Dr Pollard's inspiration has made more progress during the past twenty years than in the whole century which divides his Sandars Lectures from the death of Malone in 1812; his own *Richard II: a new quarto* furnishing at once a standard and an exemplar for all later editors.   In this progress the herculean labours, profound bibliographical knowledge, and ruthless analytical genius of Dr W. W. Greg have played a conspicuous part, while his lecture on *Principles of Emendation in Shakespeare* delivered before the British Academy in 1928 gives us a measure of the ground covered in one section of the field.   I have already acknowledged my debt to this lecture and its copious appendices, and the extent of the debt will be evident in later chapters of this book.   Here I wish only to quote one sentence. "The central point", writes Dr Greg, "at which I am aiming is this: that no emendation can, or ought to be, considered *in vacuo,* but that criticism must always proceed in relation to what we know, or what we surmise, respecting the history of the text."[1]   If under the term "emendation" be included alteration of any kind, not merely in words but also in punctuation, stage-direction and line-division, and not merely alteration of reading but choice between alternative readings present in the original texts; if in short we substitute "editorial decision" for

[1] *Emendation,* p. 8; *Aspects,* p. 133.

"emendation", as I believe Dr Greg would allow us to do, then I may claim his "central point" as my own central principle, of which the book that follows is an illustration.

§ II. THE SIX "ANCIENT COPIES"

I propose to concentrate in this enquiry upon what are now called the two "good" *Hamlet* texts, that is to say the primary editions of Q2 and F1. But before attempting to bring to the test of bibliography the vague impressions concerning these two texts of the pre-Pollardian editors just spoken of, it is necessary to define the position in general terms as regards the other texts that have come down to us from Shakespeare's day. Ultimately no theory of any one or more of the relevant texts can be satisfactory unless it is found to be consistent with a general hypothesis explaining them all, and no such general hypothesis is yet available. Nevertheless, if we can arrive at provisional conclusions about the secondary texts, they should assist us in our investigation of the primary ones. We shall be wise, therefore, to take stock of the whole field, so far as it has been surveyed, before sinking our shafts at the chosen spot. Subsequent digging may lead us to modify these provisional conclusions in detail; but fortunately, as things are, it is unlikely to do so to any serious degree.

As everyone knows, the earliest recorded reference to *Hamlet* in the history of publishing was an entry on July 26th, 1602, to James Roberts in the Stationers' Register of "A booke called the Revenge of Hamlett Prince [of] Denmarke as yt was latelie Acted by the Lord Chamberleyne his servantes". Between this entry and the appearance of F1 in 1623 four editions of the play in quarto were sold in the London booksellers' shops. These were the Q1 of 1603, known as the bad quarto, the good Q2 of 1605 which took its place, and two reprints of this latter, one undated and one dated 1611, but both published by John Smethwick who acquired rights in the book in 1607 from Nicholas Ling, the publisher of the texts of 1603 and 1605. In addition to these English publications there is a German *Hamlet*, entitled *Der bestrafte Brudermord*, the earliest form of which is a manuscript dating from 1710, but which, according to Sir Edmund Chambers, is probably derived from a *Hamlet* played in Germany by "English comedians" in the early seventeenth century.[1] Thus, including the *Hamlet* of F1, there are six texts to be reckoned with at the outset of the enquiry.

Let us deal first with the Smethwick quartos. These are mere reprints of the 1605 version, that is to say they simply reproduce the good quarto without change beyond the crop of fresh errors inevitable to the somewhat careless press-work of that age. They tell us nothing new, therefore, about Q2, and if it can be shown that they have no bearing upon the F1 text, they can be neglected. If, on the other hand, as happened with many other Shakespearian plays, the copy handled by the printers of 1623 were one of these later reprints collated by some scribe with the prompt-book in use at the Globe, then the Smethwick quartos would become of importance to an editor. Obviously the matter can only be decided by a close scrutiny of the F1 text, but the point furnishes an excellent example of the benefits of a preliminary glance at the field as a whole. The existence of the reprints is at once a warning and a guide to our investigation of F1. Indeed, one of the capital problems of that text is its bibliographical relation to those already in print. A recent critic, for example, has maintained that the Q2 of 1605 was printed from Shakespeare's manuscript; that no other manuscript ever existed; that a copy of the quarto was used as the Globe prompt-book, after being corrected from players' parts made out from the original manuscript and augmented with fresh stage-directions; and

---

[1] *Vide* Chambers, *Elizabethan Stage*, II, 285–86.

finally that the prompt-book thus corrected and augmented found its way to Jaggard's printing-house and became the copy for the F1 text.[1] The theory runs directly counter to Aldis Wright's conclusion already quoted, a conclusion which, as we shall discover, is correct. But pronouncements however absolute by an editor however distinguished are no security. Until we know exactly what the F1 text is, such theories cannot be rebutted; we are "bound in to saucy doubts and fears"; we possess no criterion even for dealing with the 1605 Q2 and its reprints.

Turning to the pirated Q1 of 1603, we may notice that in striking contrast with their vagueness and lack of curiosity as regards the texts that matter most, editors and critics have displayed a remarkable interest in this bad quarto. The great men of the eighteenth century knew nothing about it, since it first came to light in 1821, and I sometimes think that, fascinating puzzle as it is, that very fascination has been a contributory cause of the slow progress with the main textual problems. At any rate it has given editors something to write about in their introductions. While the Cambridge editors dismiss the relation between F1 and Q2 in sixteen lines, they devote two and a half pages to Q1; and the disparity is even more glaring in their introduction to the Clarendon *Hamlet*. Again in the Arden *Hamlet* Dowden gives over three times more space to Q1 than he does to the better texts. Perhaps, however, Furnivall is the worst offender. Presented with the unique opportunity of having to write an introduction to the Griggs facsimile of Q2, and beginning auspiciously enough with the words "The Second Quarto of *Hamlet* has never yet had justice done it by the Shakespeare-reading public of England", he himself flies in the face of that justice by almost immediately after going off at a tangent to discourse in characteristic vein upon Q1 for a dozen pages. If only he had deputed the writing of the

[1] De Groot, *Hamlet, its Textual History*, p. 21.

introduction to that pioneer bibliographer, P. A. Daniel, the subsequent history of *Hamlet* textual criticism might have been very different. As it is, since Furnivall's day the tide of interest in the bad quarto has shown no sign of abatement. The world loves an obvious mystery which seems to baffle solution. There are ten times as many books on the *Sonnets* as on *King Lear*, twenty times more notes on the "dram of eale" than on any other passage in *Hamlet*, and great monographs continue to appear from the presses of England, America, Holland and Italy on the mystery of Q1, while the far more vital and—if the mystery-mongers only knew it—no less fascinating, mysteries of Q2 and F1 pass almost unnoticed.[1]

But I have myself lived in glass houses and had my share in the game of bad quartos, though I do not propose to invite readers to join me in it here. Nor do I think that either the bad quarto or the *Brudermord* is unimportant, or that the work done upon them is waste labour. As I have said, all the original *Hamlet* texts hang together, and must in the end find some common historical solution. But the bad texts can never be fully understood until we know what we are dealing with in the good ones. In other words, a bibliographical enquiry into the character of the good texts must precede any final enquiry into the history of the *Hamlet* texts as a whole. And yet, just as we must keep a weather eye upon the Smethwick reprints when we come to deal with the F1 text, so we must be alive to possible bibliographical connections between Q1 and Q2. Further-more, we know enough about Q1 to make it useful in other ways. There are still almost as many theories of its origin and composition as there are critics who write about it; but they all, I think, nowadays agree upon one point, namely,

[1] Even where they receive treatment, even elaborate treatment, as at the hands of van Dam and de Groot (*vide* Preface, p. xvii), that treatment is liable to become confused and diffuse through over-much preoccupation with the problem of Q1.

that however this strange thing "of shreds and patches" came into being, its main source was not any manuscript by Shakespeare but a memorial reconstruction of his play by some person or persons, whether actors or note-taking spectators, who were present at performances of it in 1603 or shortly before. Concurrence of opinion here makes it possible to employ the debased text as a kind of control in our investigation of the other versions, since it means that when a reading in Q1 is in substantial, if not actually in verbal, agreement with the corresponding reading in either Q2 or F1, there is a *prima facie* probability that the said reading was current at performances in the Globe, though it by no means follows, let me add, that the reading is what Shakespeare himself intended.[1]

As for Q2, since Dr Pollard began his revolutionary studies of good quartos in general, there has grown up a fairly widespread and well-attested opinion that the 1605 *Hamlet*, which bears all the marks of a respectable origin, was printed direct from Shakespeare's autograph manuscript. At the same time it has come to be commonly assumed that the copy for the F1 text, if as Aldis Wright alleged "an independent manuscript", was probably a prompt-book from the playhouse. Indeed, in his *Principles of Emendation in Shakespeare*, Dr Greg adopts this twin theory to account for the two main texts and makes it the basis of his argument, though he is careful to state that he does so without necessarily accepting it. It will be convenient to follow Dr Greg's example at the outset of our enquiry and make the double assumption in order to see how far it will take us. Now, there is one thing that may be said at once about this assumption: the business end of it is that which affects F1. For if it can be shown that the text of 1623 was printed from a manuscript which was not in Shakespeare's autograph, we thereby tend to increase the presumption in favour of direct descent for Q2. We shall be wise, therefore,

[1] *Vide* Appendix A for a list of these readings.

to begin our investigation by an examination of the F1 *Hamlet*, while that examination in turn may well begin with a consideration of its more obvious characteristics, some of which have long been well known and assigned to theatrical influence, though others appear to have escaped notice hitherto.

CHAPTER II

The Character of the Folio *Hamlet*

§ III. THE GLOBE PROMPT-BOOK

(a) Playhouse abridgment

What most struck nineteenth-century editors about the F1 *Hamlet* was the absence from it of lengthy passages which had to be supplied from Q2, and they explained such omissions as theatrical cuts. These editors appear to have been unaware that omission is a general malady of the 1623 text, as it is also of the 1605 text; that each version is pitted with holes, so to speak, which can only be filled in by borrowing words, phrases, and often whole lines or groups of lines, from the other. It is clear, moreover, that the bulk of these omissions were accidental; that is to say, they had nothing to do with the needs of playhouse performances, and must therefore be set to the account of a careless scribe or compositor. Take, for example, the following from F1 (1.2.57–61):

> *King.* Haue you your Fathers leaue? What sayes Pollonius?
> *Pol.* He hath my Lord:
> I do beseech you giue him leaue to go.

Here two and a half lines have been omitted, as Q2 proves by reading:

> *King.* Haue you your fathers leaue, what saies Polonius?
> *Polo.*[1] Hath my Lord wroung from me my slowe leaue
> By laboursome petition, and at last
> Vpon his will I seald my hard consent,
> I doe beseech you giue him leaue to goe.

[1] The word "he" or "a" (=he) has been omitted here or absorbed into the "Polo".

And that the lines were almost certainly omitted by accident is shown by the Q1 version:

> *King*. Haue you your fathers leaue, Leartes?
> *Cor*. He hath, my lord, wrung from me a forced graunt,
> And I beseech you grant your Highnesse leaue,

which, being patently a memorised report of the fuller text, proves that the two and a half lines absent in F1 must have stood in the original prompt-book and have been spoken on the Globe stage. Similarly, at 4.3.27–30, F1 omits two brief speeches which appear thus in Q2:

> *King*. Alas, alas.
> *Ham*. A man may fish with the worme that hath eate of a King, & eate of the fish that hath fedde of that worme.

And once again the travesty of Hamlet's words in the Q1, which prints,

> Looke you, a man may fish with that worme
> That hath eaten of a King,
> And a Beggar eate that fish,
> Which that worme hath caught,

proves that the Globe prompt-book corresponded with the Q2 text at this point.

These examples, which illustrate the value of Q1 as a control in dealing with the better texts, bid us beware of attributing omissions in F1 too lightly to deliberate excision in preparation for stage-performance. Nevertheless, no candid student will, I think, refuse to admit that most of the remaining passages of any length which appear in Q2 and not F1 have been cut out of the latter text by, or at the instance of, someone in the theatre charged with the duty of making out a prompt-book and players' parts, who found it necessary to lighten the play, in order to shorten the length of performance, to remove what seemed to him extraneous matter, to rid the text of tangles or cruxes, and perhaps to relieve the player taking the exceedingly heavy

part of Hamlet. In the last connection, it is worth noticing
that of the 229 lines omitted from F1 no less than 171
belong either to Hamlet's part or to dialogue in which his
part is involved.

As to what I call tangles, there can be little doubt that
occasionally Shakespeare, because his imagination raced
ahead of his pen, because he grew tired, or simply because,
like the humblest author of us all, he was gravelled, not for
matter—that never seemed to fail him—but for the appropriate word or phrase, left passages behind him in the
process of composition that needed straightening out or
pruning afterwards. Readers of this book who believe, as
I do, in the Shakespearian authorship of three autograph
pages, concerned with a riot quelled by the eloquence of
More, in the old play-book entitled *The Booke of Sir Thomas
Moore* at the British Museum, will no doubt have observed
that just such a tangle occurs on the third of those pages,
and that it has been dealt with in summary fashion by a
second writer, who was presumably the prompter or book-
holder. Aware that such a person would go over the play
carefully before it was performed, in order to prepare
players' parts and perhaps a prompt-book, Shakespeare
probably troubled his head very little about his tangles. If
he remembered them, or remembering thought it worth
while, he might go back and straighten them out himself;
if not, there was always the prompter to clean up after him,
and it was part of his job to do so. Then, too, he sometimes
made blunders or wrote a word illegibly, in either case
leaving behind him a problem which, if the prompter
was unable to cope with it effectively, remained a crux for
the exercise of editorial ingenuity. Tangles and cruxes are
not uncommon in Shakespearian texts, whether in quarto
or folio, but no other text, as far as I am aware, has nearly
so many of them as *Hamlet*, a significant fact we shall have
to face later.[1]

[1] *Vide* below, pp. 90–2.

With these considerations in mind, and as already stated assuming for the purpose of the argument that Q2 is nearer to Shakespeare's original than F1, I shall now briefly survey those omissions from the latter text which may be set down as in all probability playhouse cuts. The earliest (1.1.108–25) is a passage of eighteen lines in the opening scene, comprising Horatio's speech about portents in Rome and Denmark, together with four lines by Barnardo leading up to it. On the face of it, it does nothing to help the action, and the whole thing might well have seemed to a stage-manager a rather tiresome digression, while the fact that it concludes with a derangement of some kind which no editor has since been able to rectify[1] would not tend to increase his affection for it. And the next omitted passage (1.4.17–38) is strikingly similar in character, being Hamlet's disquisition on drunkenness in Denmark and on "vicious moles of nature" in particular men, which extends to twenty-two lines and terminates with the "dram of eale" crux, the most famous of its kind in the whole Shakespearian canon. Yet, if it was the presiding genius at the Globe who found these digressions otiose, and struck them out, one may fancy, with somewhat impatient pen, they had a point—a good theatrical point—which he missed, it seems, altogether. For what follows at the end of both passages in Q2? A stage-direction—*Enter Ghost!* In other words, Shakespeare quite deliberately wrote a score or so of lines in a minor key just before the entrance of the Ghost in both scenes, in order—not to work off superabundant poetic energy—but to lull the minds of his audience to rest and so startle them the more with his apparition.

At the very outset of our enquiry, therefore, we seem to catch sight of a fundamental distinction between the two texts under consideration. It is not, as Dowden put it, that the F1 text is "more theatrical but less literary than the text of 1605"; it is not even that the one is theatrical and the

---

[1] *Vide* vol. II, pp. 222–24.

other dramatic. The real contrast is between two kinds of stage-sense. Behind F1 stands a man of the theatre with notions of stage-craft that are conventional, downright, a little crude; behind Q2 a man, no less of the theatre, capable of stage-craft so delicate and subtle that his colleague of the F1 text often misses his points altogether, though had he tried them out on the boards they would indubitably have been highly effective. It is only fair to add that the second cut from Act 1 may conceivably deserve a better excuse. For so broad a reference to the toping habits of the Danish court would perhaps have been unseemly, not to say dangerous, after 1603, when James I and his Danish consort ascended the throne.[1] Indeed, from what we know of the manners of the English court at this time, it may even have run the risk of being taken for personal reflection upon the reigning monarchs themselves. But if these were the motives that actuated the abridger in this instance, the cut must have been made in post-Elizabethan years.

A little later on in the same scene three and a half lines (1.4.75–8), describing the downward view from "the dreadful summit of the cliff", are omitted from F1. There is nothing corresponding to them in Q1; but apart from abridgment there seems no point in their omission,[2] and I suggest that they were either left out of the prompt-book by accident or, like the passages cited above, were just overlooked by the F1 compositor. Similarly there are lines omitted, no doubt accidentally, since Q1 preserves traces of them, at 2.2.17, 465–7, 487, and in other parts of the play. But the next clear indication of the playhouse pruning-knife that we encounter after the Ghost scenes is a group of small excisions in the rhyming Gonzago play (3.2.174, 181–2, 228–9). Here the results are definitely beneficial,

---

[1] Cf. below, p. 98.
[2] Delius conjectured that the lines were omitted because their substance, in an enlarged and elaborated form, was needed for the description of the cliff at Dover in *King Lear* (*vide* Furness).

may indeed have been intended by Shakespeare, and certainly could hardly have been reprehended by him; for we can imagine that he became bored with the writing of this stilted stuff. Further, the first of the omitted lines, which stands by itself in Q2 without its rhyme-pair, is probably part of one of those tangles referred to above, since there is also something wrong with the next line but one in Q2. Indeed, place the passages in the two texts side by side thus:

Q2

For women feare too much, euen as they loue,
And womens feare and loue hold quantitie,
Eyther none, in neither ought, or in extremitie

F1

For womens Feare and Loue, holds quantitie,
In neither ought, or in extremity

—and it becomes clear that the F1 version represents a successful piece of tidying up. Not merely has a superfluous line been got rid of, after the conjunction "for" has been transferred to the next line, but "eyther none", apparently a false start on Shakespeare's part, has been deleted. And when F1 omits another couple of lines almost immediately after, lines that merely repeat in substance what has already been said, we cannot withhold our sympathy from the exciser. Nor do we feel that anything is lost by the deletion, forty-five lines later, of the couplet

To desperation turne my trust and hope,
And Anchors cheere in prison be my scope,

since once again they are little more than repetitions of what precedes and follows them. The truth is, Shakespeare set himself to write an empty playlet composed of a number of moral commonplaces, and succeeded only too well.

Another group of cuts, this time longer and extending in all to twenty-six lines, comes from the scene in Gertrude's

bedroom (3.4.71–81, 161–70, 180, 202–10). For the last,
which sacrifices Hamlet's confident anticipation of being
able to deal with Rosencrantz and Guildenstern when
they reach England, one can imagine no reason except
a desire to economise lines in the Hamlet part. The cuts
in the first two passages are at once more explicable and
less injurious, since the deleted matter consists of difficult
and somewhat obscure observations of a psychological
character on the senses, which we can surrender without
any feeling of dramatic loss. In both, too, the knife has
been handled in such a way as hardly at all to disturb the
metrical arrangement, while it has spared a brief passage in
the very midst of the rejected material. In a word, the
excisions are at once deft and considerate. But their nature
and quality can be best appreciated with the passages in
front of one. I therefore quote both, as they appear in Q2,
but picking out the portions omitted from F1 by means of
italics. Here is the first:

> You cannot call it loue, for at your age
> The heyday in the blood is tame, it's humble,
> And waits vppon the iudgement, and what iudgement   70
> Would step from this to this, *sence sure youe haue*
> *Els could you not haue motion, but sure that sence*
> *Is appoplext, for madnesse would not erre*
> *Nor sence to extacie was nere so thral'd*
> *But it reseru'd some quantity of choise*   75
> *To serue in such a difference,* what deuill wast
> That thus hath cosund you at hodman blind;
> *Eyes without feeling, feeling without sight,*
> *Eares without hands, or eyes, smelling sance all,*
> *Or but a sickly part of one true sence*   80
> *Could not so mope:* ô shame where is thy blush?
> Rebellious hell,
> If thou canst mutine in a Matrons bones, etc.

It will be noticed that the cut leaves the second part of l. 76
to follow neatly upon the first part of l. 71 without any

break in the metre, while the second half of l. 81 is attached
to the broken l. 82 in F1, thus:

> O shame! where is thy Blush? Rebellious Hell,

which likewise makes a satisfactory line of verse. Turning
to the other passage, it should be remarked that here the
impelling motive of the cut was apparently as much difficulty of handwriting in the original as difficulty of meaning,
since the lines in Q2 contain two bad cruxes, one of them
caused perhaps by the omission of a word. Thus it runs:

> Assume[1] a vertue if you haue it not,   160
> *That monster custome, who all sence doth eate*
> *Of habits deuill, is angell yet in this*
> *That to the vse of actions faire and good,*
> *He likewise giues a frock or Liuery*
> *That aptly is put on* refraine to night,[2]   165
> And that shall lend a kind of easines
> To the next abstinence, *the next more easie:*
> *For vse almost can change the stamp of nature,*
> *And either the deuill, or throwe him out*
> *With wonderous potency:* once more good night,   170
> And when you are desirous to be blest, etc.

Here the metre has not escaped quite so successfully as in
the other instance. The words "refraine to night" have
been left in mid-air and are tacked on to the end of l. 160
in F1. Nevertheless, once again we cannot help being
struck with the delicacy and skill of the operation. It was
no careless reader, or thoughtless hand, which went out of
its way to spare those middle portions; it would have been
so easy just to run a pen through the whole thing. We may
deplore or condemn the F1 cuts; we cannot say they were
made without careful consideration. Shakespeare himself
could hardly have pruned his own verse more tenderly.

A special interest belongs to the next passage to be dealt

----

[1] Q2 misprints this "Assune".
[2] Q2 misprints "to refraine night".

with—a small detached cut at 4.1.40–44, inasmuch as the
first half-line of it is omitted from Q2 also, so that the
substance of this half-line has to be supplied by the ingenuity
of editors. Here is the passage in its context:

> And let them know both what we meane to doe
> And whats vntimely doone,   40
> *Whose whisper ore the worlds dyameter,*
> *As leuell as the Cannon to his blanck,*
> *Transports his poysned shot, may misse our Name,*
> *And hit the woundlesse ayre,* ô come away,
> My soule is full of discord and dismay.   45

Three alternative explanations seem possible for this phenomenon: (i) that the missing half of l. 40 was accidentally
omitted by the transmitters of both texts; (ii) that it was
missing in the manuscript which lies behind both texts,
in other words that Shakespeare himself left it out, which
would in turn explain why the whole passage, brief and
harmless enough in itself, came to be cut in F1; and (iii) that
the lines in question were marked for omission in the
original manuscript not by transverse lines of deletion but
by some kind of brackets or rectangular enclosure, an arm
of which accidentally appeared to delete the first half-line
of the passage, so that the Q2 compositor set up all but that
half-line. It is one of the few instances in *Hamlet* of a
"depravation" which is hopelessly beyond repair, and we
have to content ourselves with "so haply slander" which
Theobald and Capell devised between them—a makeshift,
but a happy one.

Next follows the longest and best known omission of all,
that of the fourth soliloquy, together with the dialogue
between Hamlet and the Norwegian captain which in-
troduces it (4.4.9–66). It is an obvious cut made for
theatrical purposes; it not only saves fifty-eight lines, but
a considerable quantity of Burbadge's breath. Moreover,
as some critics have supposed that the fourth soliloquy may

have been an addition to the play by Shakespeare after the performances of 1601 and the construction of the original prompt-book, it may be observed that the Fortinbras scene was patently written in order to give occasion to the soliloquy and that the scene (without the soliloquy) is reported in Q1. It follows from this that Fortinbras and his army, together with Hamlet's soliloquy, were in the completed text from the very first, but that the soliloquy was omitted from the prompt-book also from the first.

The long scene between Claudius and Laertes, in which the plot against Hamlet is laid and the fencing-match arranged, contains yet another group of cuts (4.7.69–82, 101–3, 115–24), running in all to twenty-six lines. The theatre loses nothing by their omission; the first expressing the King's rather old-fashioned views upon duelling, the second consisting of a couple of lines upon "scrimers" in France, and the third being a gnomic passage built up round a somewhat far-fetched quibble on the word "plurisy". It may be said, in short, that if twenty-six lines had to be sacrificed in this scene, the choice was well made.

Finally, we come to a pair of longish cuts in the last scene of the play (5.2.110–50, 203–18). The first of them abridges the Osric episode and throws overboard that fop's very difficult description of Laertes, together with Hamlet's scarcely less difficult rejoinder. In this the abridger has our understanding if not our sympathy, while once again his manner of going to work shows the craftsman's hand. Indeed, it is in this cut, of all the cuts in the text, that the presence of his hand is most unmistakable. To have deleted forty-one lines and done no more would have broken the thread of the dialogue, since it would have removed all reference to Laertes and his weapon, and so left what follows without meaning. The abridger accordingly mended his rent by reading "Sir, you are not ignorant of what excellence Laertes is at his weapon", a sentence which does not actually occur in Q2, though every word of it is Shakespeare's. As for the other cut, it possesses the theatrical merit of saving a part, seeing that it altogether suppresses the lord, who follows Osric and does nothing but repeat the message and the question with which the latter had been charged. Shakespeare probably introduced this lord in order to show us that when Osric "re-delivered" Hamlet's reply to the King, the latter found him even more difficult to follow than Hamlet had, and was therefore forced to send a second emissary to discover his meaning. But the Osric business is over-long in any event, and it is difficult not to regard the F1 cut as a definite improvement. The only serious loss is the message from the Queen bidding Hamlet "use some gentle entertainment to Laertes" before they "fall to play".

Our review of the cuts in *Hamlet* F1 has clearly revealed the hand of a stage-adapter in that text, and has given us a little information concerning him. While the subtler intentions of Shakespeare seem to escape him, there is nothing slap-dash or slovenly about him. We have seen how careful he is to save a line here or a line there which he thinks effective, and how neatly he can mend a rent in the text when need be. Further, his choice of material to be sacrificed is on the whole judicious. If 229 lines had to be cut out of *Hamlet*, in order to bring the play within manageable lengths for performance, it would not be easy to suggest another 229 as suitable as those he selected for rejection. In short, (if he was not Shakespeare himself) he must have been a competent person; not perhaps according to modern standards respectful enough to a Shakespearian text, though many modern managers show far less respect, but certainly an experienced stage-hand qualified to prepare any ordinary play-book for performance. It is natural to suppose—more especially as the copy for F1 came from the Globe playhouse—that this businesslike fellow was none other than the prompter at that theatre, or rather the prompter who presided over the

Globe round about 1601 when the original prompt-copy must have been made out.

For it is probable that most of these cuts were to be found in the acting version right from the first. And it is worth noting in this connection that wherever we can use the bad Q1 as control it offers no evidence that the deleted passages were being spoken on the stage when that pirated text was being composed, that is to say, in 1602 or 1603. Though, for instance, as we have seen, traces are to be found of those two and a half lines of Polonius's first speech in act 1, scene 2, which were omitted from F1 by inadvertence, there is nothing whatever in Q1 to correspond with the digressions on portents and drunkenness in the Ghost scenes; and yet as every student of that text knows those scenes are better reported than any other. Nevertheless, such evidence must not be pressed too far. While the presence in Q1 of any version, however debased, of a passage which is found in one of the two good texts but not in the other is virtual proof that that passage was once spoken on the stage and was presumably part of the prompt-copy, the absence of any passage from the reported text is at best negative evidence.

(b) Stage-directions and speech-headings[1]

If the cuts in F1 suggest a playhouse scribe preparing the text for performance, even stronger evidence pointing in that direction is afforded by the stage-directions, which differ throughout from those of Q2. Indeed, one has only to compare the two versions in this respect to be convinced, I think, that while the Q2 stage-directions are Shakespeare's, those of F1 must have been penned by someone who, though often introducing technical improvements and clarifications, even more often blurred or obliterated the

[1] *Vide* Appendix D for a Comparative Table of Stage-directions and Speech-headings.

author's dramatic purposes. The cuts may conceivably have been made by the author, acting under instruction; the stage-directions cannot possibly be his.

As good an example of this as any is found in the direction which opens the second scene of the play. Here Q2 reads, if we remove a couple of simple misprints:

> *Florish. Enter Claudius, King of Denmarke, Gertrud[1] the Qyeene, Counsailors,[1] Polonius, and his Sonne Laertes, Hamlet, Cum Alijs.*

Two points may be noted about this: (1) that a meeting of the King's Council is taking place, the first indeed to transact business since the combined marriage and coronation festivities, and (2) that Hamlet, in mourning and with downcast mien, enters last of a brilliant procession in gala costume, against which his black figure shows up in startling contrast. Both these effects are ignored in F1, which gives us:

> *Enter Claudius King of Denmarke, Gertrude the Qyeene, Hamlet, Polonius, Laertes, and his Sister Ophelia, Lords Attendant.*

Thus Hamlet is brought in, in strict order of court precedence, next his mother, the Council disappears, and Ophelia is added in order to complete the Polonius family party; changes which at once ruin the colour-scheme and deprive the scene of its political significance. And there is a further change which has quite definitely been made in the interests of stage-convenience. The chief business of the Council meeting is the threat from Norway and young Fortinbras, together with the dispatch of ambassadors to deal with it. No ambassadors are specifically mentioned in the Q2 direction; they are included among the "Counsailors". F1, on the other hand, gives them an entry by name, not however at the head of the scene, but twenty-five lines from its commencement, after Claudius has already been talking

---

[1] Q2 prints "Gertrad" and "Counsaile:as".

about Fortinbras for ten lines, and only just in the nick of time to receive their commission. This tardy entry can best be explained, I think, by some necessity of the tiring-room; I suggest, in short, that Cornelius and Valtemand had been playing Marcellus and Barnardo in the previous scene and needed the twenty-five lines for a hurried change of costume. And Q1, which begins the scene at the exact point marked for their entry in F1, lends support to this hypothesis.[1]

Similar changes to those at the head of 1.2 may be found in 4.3, which opens with a speech by Claudius discussing what should be done with Hamlet after the murder of Polonius, a speech which is clearly intended to be addressed to confidential advisers and is duly, if vaguely, headed in Q2, *Enter King, and two or three*. This F1, by reading *Enter King* in order to save two or three supers, turns into a soliloquy, and thus misses the whole point of the speech. On the other hand, as I have said, many of the changes make for simplicity and clarification. Thus, to continue with the same scene, at the end of the King's speech Q2 gives the direction, *Enter Rosencrans*[2] *and all the rest* which becomes *Enter Rosincrane* in F1, while a few lines later, at the King's command that Hamlet should be brought before him, Q2 reads:

> *Ros.* How, bring in the Lord.   *They enter.*

and F1:

> *Rosen.* Hoa, Guildensterne? Bring in my Lord.
>   *Enter Hamlet and Guildensterne.*

This example shows that the author of the F1 directions did not shrink from altering the text itself, when it was necessary to adapt it to suit his stage-arrangements. Yet the gain in clarity of stage-situation effected by the change

---

[1] The inference being that the pirate responsible for the Q1 text played one of the ambassadors and, being in the tiring-room at the opening of the scene, was unable to secure copy for those twenty-five lines.

[2] Q2 prints this name "Rosencraus" throughout.

cannot be disputed, and even the disturbance of the text is harmless.

A like tolerance is not, however, to be extended to a parallel piece of adaptation which occurs at 1.5.113, after the exit of the Ghost and Hamlet's solemn oath to keep faith with it. I quote Q2, and may remind the reader that, the time being shortly after midnight, the speakers are in darkness, groping their way about the stage, and that at first Hamlet is still on his knees after taking the oath.

> *Enter Horatio, and Marcellus.*
>
> *Hora.* My Lord, my Lord.
> *Mar.* Lord Hamlet.
> *Hora.* Heauens secure him.
> *Ham.* So be it.
> *Mar.* Illo, ho, ho, my Lord.
> *Ham.* Hillo, ho, ho, boy come, bird,[1] come.

F1 rewrites the whole thing:

> *Hor. & Mar. within.* My Lord, my Lord.
>
> *Enter Horatio and Marcellus.*
>
> *Mar.* Lord Hamlet.
> *Hor.* Heauen secure him.
> *Mar.* So be it.
> *Hor.* Illo, ho, ho, my Lord.
> *Ham.* Hillo, ho, ho, boy; come bird, come.

The rearrangement gives "So be it" to Marcellus and "Illo, ho, ho, my Lord" to Horatio. The second transference matters little, but the first is inexcusable, since, as Capell long ago remarked, "there is something highly solemn and proper in making Hamlet say amen to a benediction pronounced on himself". And yet quite a number of modern editors have not hesitated to follow F1, while even the level-headed Furness refuses to decide between the readings.

[1] "bird" is misprinted "and" in Q2.

A scarcely less unhappy redistribution of speeches may be found in the first twenty-five lines of the play, where Q2 gives the contemptuous question, "What, ha's this thing appeard againe to night?" to the sceptical Horatio, and F1 transfers it, perhaps in order to ease the give-and-take of the dialogue, to Marcellus. But the most striking and important change of the kind, though it has hitherto I believe passed entirely unnoticed, is that which substituted the word "Priest" for the abbreviation "Doct." as the prefix to the speeches of the "churlish priest" at Ophelia's funeral.[1] Shakespeare's intention, preserved in the Q2 prefix "Doct." which I take for "Doctor of Divinity", was, I do not doubt, that the "maiméd rites" should be conducted by a Protestant minister in black gown and cassock. The F1 change has not merely obscured this for over three centuries, but has opened the door to the *Priests, etc. in procession* of modern editors, the "*etc.*" being a hint to stage-managers for a cross and censers, to say nothing of other apparatus of Catholic ritual.

"Priests in procession", however, though they must be laid indirectly to the account of F1, are by no means characteristic of that text, one mark of which, as we have already observed, is economy of man-power. Q2 provides two English ambassadors at the end of the play; F1 reduces them to one. In 4.6 Q2 reads *Enter Saylers* and F1 *Enter Saylor*. Yet again, in the conversation between Hamlet and his two school-fellows after the play-scene, Q2 prints *Enter the Players with Recorders* and gives Hamlet the exclamation, "ô, the Recorders, let mee see one", which in F1 have become *Enter one with a Recorder* and "O the Recorder. Let me see". Such changes are innocent enough, if a little cheese-paring; but manhandling Shakespeare is a dangerous business—as every editor is aware—and the person responsible for these alterations is always liable to trip. He certainly does so in 4.5 which is headed *Enter Horatio*,

[1] 5.1.249, 258.

Gertrard, and a Gentleman in Q2. In his eagerness to save
a part, he cuts out the Gentleman, giving his two speeches
to Horatio and Horatio's speech to the Queen. This is
unfortunate, since the whole point of Horatio's presence in
the scene is to show him as the guardian of Hamlet's
honour which, as the Gentleman hints broadly, Ophelia's
mad talk is calling in question; yet F1 puts the Gentleman's
innuendoes into Horatio's mouth! On the other hand, a
piece of adaptation in 4.1 is once again a definite improvement. The scene, following immediately on the conversation in the bedroom between Hamlet and his mother, which
leaves the Queen weeping and distraught upon the stage,
is oddly headed in Q2 *Eenter King, and Queene, with Rosencraus and Guyldensterne*; oddly, I say, for not only is an
entry for the Queen superfluous when she is already "on",
but Rosencrantz and Guildenstern are quite obviously in
the way, so much so that the Queen has to get rid of them
at once by bidding them "Bestow this place on vs a little
while". How this awkward situation arose is a Q2 problem
which does not concern us at the moment.[1] What we have
to notice is the simple and efficient manner in which F1
deals with it: it reads *Enter King* and cuts out Rosencrantz
and Guildenstern together with the words addressed to
them. To my mind had we no other evidence than this, we
should be justified in concluding that the F1 text was in
some way derived from acting copy.

We have seen above that, if the deletion of Hamlet's
reference to the drinking habits of the Danish court at
1.4.17–38 was prompted by political reasons, it must have
been made after the accession of James and at some date
therefore subsequent to the original construction of the
prompt-book. Are there any F1 stage-directions which
point to Jacobean interference with the text? There is,
I think, at least one clear instance, though it has nothing

[1] *Vide* pp. 91–2.

to do with politics. The direction at 5.2.235 runs as
follows in the two main texts:

Q2

*A table prepard, Trumpets, Drums and officers with Cushions,
King, Queene, and all the state, Foiles, daggers,
and Laertes.*

F1

*Enter King, Queene, Laertes and Lords, with other Atten-
dants with Foyles, and Gauntlets, a Table and
Flagons of Wine on it.*

In 1605, it will be noticed, we have foils and daggers; in
1623, foils and gauntlets; and the difference marks a change
in the fashion of fencing which had taken place during the
interval. At the end of the sixteenth and the beginning of
the seventeenth century it was customary to fence with
rapier and dagger, the latter being held in the left hand and
used to ward off thrusts on the left. But the practice did not
last long in Stuart England, and was superseded by "single
rapier play", while on the now disengaged left hand was
worn a leather gauntlet.[1] The purpose of this gauntlet was
not defence, which was now effected by the rapier alone,
but to enable the fencer to seize his opponent's sword and
wrest it out of his hand, if opportunity offered.

It is clear from the text itself that Shakespeare planned
the sword-play between Hamlet and Laertes to be one with
rapier and dagger, since the whole of Osric's conversation
with Hamlet just beforehand turns upon the fact. The
theatre, however, must ever change with the times, and
we can feel pretty certain that the F1 direction represents
an attempt to keep up-to-date. It follows that the alteration
must have been made, not at the time of the construction

---

[1] *Vide* Introduction (pp. vi–viii, xi–xx) to ed. of Silver's *Paradoxes
of Defence* (Shak. Assoc.). The combatants in rapier and dagger fence
apparently wore gloves of mail on both hands.

of the original prompt-book, but some, perhaps many, years later. In other words it is Jacobean, not Elizabethan. Nor is it the only stage-direction in F1 which in all probability dates from after the accession of James I. When, for example, at the opening of the Play-scene Claudius and Gertrude enter with the court, F1 gives the direction *Danish March*, of which Q2 makes no mention, and it is natural to suppose that the words were added after the accession of James's consort, Anne of Denmark, to the throne. Indeed, before 1603 a London audience would hardly be likely to recognise the music as connected with Denmark at all.

(c) The Folio text printed from an independent manuscript

All the phenomena noted above—the playhouse cuts, the revised stage-directions, and so on—point unmistakably to playhouse interference, and go some way towards proving, or at least rendering extremely likely, the provisional theory we set out from, namely, that the F1 text was printed from some kind of copy closely associated if not actually identical with the Globe prompt-book; while the more we review its departures from the good Q2 text, the more inclined we become to perceive a close affinity between the latter and a manuscript in the hand of Shakespeare himself.

Further, the hypothesis that F1 may have been printed from a copy of Q2 which had served as prompt-book and had been adapted for performance by additions, cuts and alterations from the book-holder's hand, is discredited in advance. We shall knock the bottom out of it in the section that follows, but even now we can see that it will not hold water, and that for a very good reason. Cuts and alterations might have been made easily enough on the pages of a printed book, but how came those additions into the supposed Q2 prompt-book? There are, for example, three lengthy passages (2.2.244–76, 2.2. 352–79, 5.2.68–80) which F1 contains and Q2 does not; where did they come from? All of them, we shall later see,[1] must have stood in Shakespeare's original manuscript; and the only satisfactory way of accounting for their presence in F1 is to suppose that text independently derived from the parent manuscript. Nor are these long omissions alone in question. Q2 is, as I have already hinted, full of little omissions which have to be supplied from F1 by modern editors. There are, in fact, close on a hundred of these.[2] Once again, how did they find their way into F1, except from Shakespeare's own manuscript? If the F1 text, then, be derived from a Globe prompt-book, as we have seen it must have been, that prompt-book presented a very different text from that we find in Q2 of 1605. In other words, the copy for the F1 *Hamlet* was as Aldis Wright declared, whether he meant it or not, "an independent manuscript".

It is, of course, natural to suppose that this manuscript was nothing but the prompt-book itself; and I myself believed it to be so for some considerable time. Further investigation, however, renders this theory untenable. The copy for the F1 text was neither a quarto nor a prompt-book; it was a *tertium quid*, the nature of which will be explored in the next section.

[1] *Vide* below, pp. 96–8.
[2] *Vide* vol. II, pp. 247–51.

§ IV. THE COPY FOR *HAMLET*, 1623

(*a*) General characteristics

None of the departures from the good Q2 hitherto discussed forbids us, I have said, to suppose that the copy for the F1 *Hamlet* was a normal prompt-book belonging to the leading company of players in London. The person responsible for them often misunderstood his author's intentions or ignored them; yet he was both careful and skilful, and there is every reason for believing him to have been the book-holder for the Chamberlain's Men, whose duty it was to convert Shakespeare's draft into effective acting copy, a duty which he set about with as much competence as might be expected from a playhouse official of the kind. On the other hand, our investigation has so far proceeded a very little way and has touched the framework of the text only. It is time to go much deeper, and to attack, for example, that massive bulk of variant readings between the two good texts which has been more than once referred to but not yet scrutinised. We have, in a word, to turn now to the dialogue of the F1 *Hamlet*, and to enquire how far it can be regarded as a faithful reproduction (apart from the playhouse cuts) of Shakespeare's verse and prose.

In order to avoid any appearance of begging the question, let me begin by taking, not Q2, but the Cambridge text of 1866 as my standard; that is to say, let Aldis Wright be the judge of what is worthy or unworthy of Shakespeare. Submitted to this test, the dialogue of the F1 *Hamlet* reveals a condition of affairs, not only incredible in the prompt-book of a reputable company, but one which no allowance for low theatrical standards or personal obtuseness on the part of a book-holder can palliate. Viewed in the mass, the textual imperfections of the F1 version are "gross as a mountain, open, palpable", so palpable indeed

that they ought long ago to have been exposed and con-
demned. The truth is, as was pointed out in my first
section, that the tradition of collation has stood in the path
of any real examination of the 1623 *Hamlet* in and for
itself. The best known texts of the canon are those of which
only a single original has survived; when there are two
authoritative texts, editors have been usually too much
engaged in collating them to get any general sense of either.
Had Aldis Wright or Dowden, for example, pushed their
enquiries into the *Hamlet* texts past the impressions noted
above, had they studied the F1 text as a special phenomenon
by itself, they must have concluded that it was one of the
most corrupt of the whole Shakespearian corpus. I do not
myself know that it is absolutely the worst, because I have
not so far examined all the F1 texts. But it is certainly the
worst I have as an editor yet encountered; much worse, for
instance, than those poor specimens, *The Merry Wives*,
Measure for Measure, and *All's Well*.

To illustrate its special quality, let us compare it with
another text from F1. *Antony and Cleopatra* is not far
short in length, running, according to the latest and most
exact computation[1] to round about 3000 lines, while the
F1 *Hamlet* contains roughly 3500 lines. Furthermore, it
has earned the special opprobrium of editors who, relieved of
the necessity of collation by the absence of a second original
text, have found time to examine its defects closely. Yet,
while Aldis Wright's text in *The Cambridge Shakespeare*
departs from the F1 *Antony and Cleopatra* in about 330
readings, it does so from the F1 *Hamlet* in about 730. And
when these departures are analysed the contrast is even
more striking, as will be seen from the following table:

[1] *Vide* Alfred Hart, *The Number of Lines in Shakespeare's Plays*
(*Review of English Studies*, 1932, p. 21).

*Departures in " The Cambridge Shakespeare" from the texts
of "Antony and Cleopatra" and "Hamlet" in* F1[1]

(A)				A. and C.	Hamlet
Punctuation ...	...	...	...	87	74
Spellings (abnormal) ...	...	...		52	83
Variant pronoun forms (e.g. "my", "mine", etc.)	...	...	...	0	25
Contractions ...	...	...	...	2	30
Mistakes in names	...	...	...	44	11
Stage-directions and speech-headings ...				25	14

(B) *Normal compositors' slips:*					
(i) Literals ...	...	...	...	12	8
(ii) Misdivided words	...	...		3	3
(iii) Omitted letters ...	...	...		7	7
(iv) Inversions	...	...	...	8	15
(v) Errors in pronouns (e.g. "you" for "your", "my" for "thy", etc.) ...				8	13
(vi) Other slips	...	...	...	4	16

(C) *Errors possibly due to misreading:*					
Minim	...	...	...	...	17	20
a : minim	...	...	...	...	1	2
e : *d* ...	...	...	...	...	5	7
o : *e* ...	...	...	...	...	2	2
a : *o* ...	...	...	...	...	2	3
f : long *s*	...	...	...	...	2	3
t : *e* ...	...	...	...	...	0	1
t : *l* ...	...	...	...	...	2	0
t : *c* ...	...	...	...	...	0	0
l : *k* ...	...	...	...	...	0	3
Errors with *r* ...	...	...	...	0	6

[1] *Vide* Appendix C for a classified list of the readings in the F1
Hamlet summarised in this table. The readings in the F1 *Antony and
Cleopatra* will be found (unclassified) at the end of the facsimile of that
text published by Faber and Faber.

(D) *More serious mistakes:*

	A. and C.	Hamlet
Verbs (error in tense, mood, person, number)	13	32
Substantives (confusion between sing. and plur.)	8	47
Omitted words and phrases	6	86
Words added	0	24
Substitution of one word for another ...	20	219

The figures of the first three main groups tally pretty closely in the two texts. The large number of mistakes in names occurring in *Antony and Cleopatra* is accounted for by its being a Roman play, full of Latin names which Shakespeare himself apparently did not trouble over-much to spell correctly. On the other hand, the fact that all the variant pronoun-forms and nearly all the variant contractions are to be found in *Hamlet* is due to there being two texts of the latter, the departures in the modern text being in the main readings from Q2 preferred by editors. The quantity of compositors' slips is almost exactly equal in the two plays, and though what I have called possible errors of misreading number forty-seven in *Hamlet* to thirty-one in *Antony and Cleopatra*, the difference does not call for any particular comment, except in regard to the last item. There is certainly something that needs explaining in the following misprints in the F1 *Hamlet*:

1.2.248 treble (tenable)	3.4.152 ranke (ranker)
3.2.174 forme (former)	5.1.269 terrible woer (treble woe)
3.4.65 breath (brother)	5.2.154 wag'd (wager'd)

They have no parallel in Q2, nor as far as I know in any other good Shakespearian text; and they suggest a scribal hand very careless in the formation of the letter *r*, especially when written in conjunction with an *e*. The clue, too slight of itself to lead to any definite conclusion, becomes significant in the light of the variants under the fourth main head.

Really serious textual abnormalities have been brought together in this last group, and the difference between the two F1 plays is here most arresting. So wide indeed is the disparity that, assuming as we legitimately may that the texts were set up by compositors who were, if not the same workman, workmen at least of similar efficiency, it can only be ascribed to a fundamental difference in the copies supplied to them. Further, numerous as the errors in *Antony and Cleopatra* are, they may all be explained as misprints and misreadings of an ordinary compositor working from a manuscript in Shakespeare's autograph.[1] It is therefore difficult to avoid the suspicion that the unusual number of errors in the F1 *Hamlet* must be set down to some transcriber who intervened between Shakespeare's manuscript and the printers of 1623. To suppose, however, this copyist to be identical with the man responsible for the prompt-copy is to fly in the face of all our findings of the previous chapter. In other words, it looks as if there must be two transcripts between Shakespeare's manuscript and the F1 text. But this is only surmise, and surmise is of little service to an editor. What he needs is certainty, or at least assurance firm enough for security of footstep. This assurance may, I think, be obtained from a narrower scrutiny of the items under our fourth head.

In examining these items we must be careful to make generous allowance for the possibility of error on the part of the F1 compositors. Thus confusion of tense, person, number and mood in verbs, and confusion of number in nouns, are common types of compositors' misprint;[2] and though we can hardly believe that the F1 compositors would go astray in such matters more than three times as frequently in *Hamlet* as in *Antony and Cleopatra*, it will be safer not to build too much upon these confusions. Com-

---

[1] *Vide* my Introduction to *Antony and Cleopatra*, Folio Facsimile Texts (Faber and Faber).

[2] *Vide* p. 119, and vol. II, pp. 235-41, 299-301.

positors, again, are as prone to omit words and phrases as
copyists are; and as a matter of fact there are a larger number
of omissions in the Q2 *Hamlet*[1] than in the F1 text, so that
the eighty-six examples in the latter are not in themselves an argument for transcription, though once again it
is certainly odd to find thirteen times as many of them in
the one F1 text as in the other. It is best, therefore, to confine
our attention to the class of verbal substitutions. Here too,
however, a caveat is necessary. A number of small verbal
changes, effecting little or no obvious difference in Shakespeare's meaning, may be and indeed almost certainly are
present in the text of *Antony and Cleopatra*; though they
can never come to light because only one text of this play
has survived. Who can tell, for instance, how many more
or less innocent departures from what Shakespeare actually
wrote, such as the following in the F1 *Hamlet*: "just"
(jump), "day" (morn), "peculiar" (particular), "see thou
character" (look thou character), "wafts" (waves), form
part of the accepted text of *Antony and Cleopatra*? To
put the same thing in another way, I reckon that of the
219 verbal substitutions in the F1 *Hamlet* some 150 might
have passed muster had we no Q2 with which to check them,
though I hope that at least a few of them would become
critical storm-centres. It is a solemn thought for editors!
Fortunately, however, it need not unduly disturb editors
of *Hamlet*, seeing that here we do possess a second text, and
that we have only to compare the *Hamlet* of F1 with that
of Q2 to see at once that a large proportion of the 219 substitutions in the former are in the nature of paraphrase,
vulgarisation, or sheer misapprehension.[2]

Among examples of paraphrase five may be quoted:

I.2.11

(Q2) With an auspitious, and a dropping eye
(F1) With one Auspicious, and one Dropping eye,

---

[1] *Vide* vol. II, pp. 244–62.   [2] For full details *vide* Appendix C.

which is the kind of flashy embellishment too often found in this text.

1.3.26

(Q2) As he in his particuler act and place
(F1) As he in his peculiar Sect and force,

where the word "act" appears to have been misread "sect", which at that period might be interpreted "sex", and then "place" emended to "force" to suit the context thus created. In the other three instances F1 departs not merely from Shakespeare's words but from his metre also.

4.1.10

(Q2) Whyps out his Rapier, cryes a Rat, a Rat
(F1) He whips his Rapier out, and cries a Rat, a Rat

4.7.60

(Q2) I my Lord, so you will not ore-rule me to a peace.
(F1) If so you'l not o'rerule me to a peace

Here a modern text would of course read:

> Ay, my lord,
> So you will not o'er-rule me to a peace,

but Q2 follows its normal method of reading a brief speech of this kind in one line, and I make little doubt that such was often Shakespeare's own practice.[1] The fifth instance is from 5.2.299:

(Q2) Heere Hamlet take my napkin rub thy browes
(F1) Heere's a Napkin, rub thy browes.

I do not think that any of these five examples of paraphrase in F1 can be set down with likelihood to the compositors of that volume, though it is possible to attribute them to carelessness or, in the case of the first and second, to deliberate alteration on the part of the Globe prompter.

Examples of vulgarisation in the F1 text, that is of tame and conventional words substituted for the poetical or pithy

---

[1] *Vide* vol. II, p. 221.

expressions of Q2, are too numerous to quote at length.[1]
Here are, however, a handful by way of illustration from
the opening scene:

Q2	F1
65 iump at this dead houre	iust at this dead houre
150 the trumpet to the morne	the Trumpet to the day
161 dare sturre abraode	can walke abroad
167 yon high Eastward hill	yon high Easterne Hill

Closely connected with this class of substitution are changes
resulting from misunderstanding. Take, for instance, this
variant:

3.3.81

(Q2) Withall his crimes braod blowne, as flush as May
(F1) With all his Crimes broad blowne, as fresh as May,

where the F1 text implies a definite misconception of the
original. Even more patent is the misunderstanding displayed by F1 at

1.2.155

(Q2) Had left the flushing in her gauled eyes
(F1) Had left the flushing of her gauled eyes.

For "flushing in" refers to the redness caused by the salt
in the eyes, while "flushing of" was presumably taken as
referring to their rinsing by the tears. The F1 text, again,
has a preference for adverbial and other forms in -*y* or -*ly*
in place of the more Shakespearian usages, a change
which at times produces surprising results. Thus we have
the variants at 1.5.18:

(Q2) Thy knotted and combined locks to part
(F1) Thy knotty and combined locks to part,

over which editors wrangle; and at 1.2.68:

(Q2) Good Hamlet cast thy nighted colour off
(F1) Good Hamlet cast thy nightly colour off,

---

[1] They are given in vol. II, p. 350.

where F1 still has some defenders, strange as it may seem; and at 1.2.240:

> (Q2) His beard was grissl'd, no
> (F1) His Beard was grisly? no

—in which F1 has clearly transferred the horror of the spectral apparition to the beard of the living man! Similarly, F1 gives us "conueniently" for "conuenient" (1.1.175), "parley" for "parle" (1.3.123), "inquiry" for "inquire" (2.1.4), "especiallý" for "especiall" (4.7.99), "royally" for "royall" (5.2.409).

Perhaps, too, we ought to include under this head absurd changes such as at 3.2.36 of "the gate[1] of Christian, Pagan, nor man" (Q2) to "the gate of Christian, Pagan, or Norman" (F1), at 4.5.146 of "Pelican" (Q2) to "Politician" (F1), or at 5.1.177 of "Sexten" (Q2) to "sixeteene" (F1), though these may be due to a compositor or press-corrector in Jaggard's office. For, once again, we must be on our guard. It is possible to contend that many of these vulgarisations and misunderstandings are printers' mistakes, and we shall certainly find some examples of the kind when we come to consider the printing of Q2. All we can say at this juncture is that if all these changes were made by Jaggard's workmen, then they must have been ten times more incompetent in dealing with *Hamlet* than they were in the printing of *Antony and Cleopatra*.

(*b*) A second transcriber detected

Let us now pass to a different class of error by substitution, a class we may label Verbal Repetition and Anticipation. It is a common failing of compositors to go astray by repeating a word they have just set up in type in place of another word, more especially if the two words possess some similarity of sound or sense; and I have noted five

---

[1] A common spelling of "gait".

examples of this in Q2, which as we shall discover is a very
badly printed book. To make the matter clear, it will be
well to quote these examples in full, with the true readings,
which this time come from F1. Their quotation collectively
will incidentally serve to explain the misprints in Q2 which,
taken individually, might otherwise be a source of puzzle-
ment to editors.

1.1.45

(F1) *Barn.* It would be spoke too.   *Mar.* Question it Horatio.
(Q2) *Bar.* It would be spoke to.   *Mar.* *Speake to* it Horatio.

2.2.389–90

(F1) Let me comply with you in the Garbe, lest my extent.
(Q2) let mee comply with you in this garb: *let me* extent.

3.4.214–15

(F1) Is now most still, most secret, and most graue,
     Who was in life, a foolish prating Knaue.
(Q2) Is now most still, most secret, and most graue,
     Who was in life a *most* foolish prating knaue.

5.1.209–13

(F1) Your flashes of Merriment that were wont to set the Table
     on a Rore?...Now get you to my Ladies Chamber
(Q2) your flashes of merriment, that were wont to set the table
     on a roare....Now get you to my Ladies *table*

4.7.192

(F1) But that this folly doubts it.
(Q2) But that this folly *drownes* it.

This last is a particularly interesting example, the substitution of "drownes" for "doubts" or "douts" being clearly
due to the influence of "drownd", which appears three
times in ll. 184–5 above. I suspect, however, that a press-
corrector was actually responsible for the change.[1]

The foregoing citations prove that compositors are
prone to repetition, and that a compositor like the in-

---

[1] *Vide* below, p. 137.

different workman who set up Q2, could commit no less than five errors of the kind in a single text. Yet it is remarkable, to say the least of it, to find that while the compositors of *Antony and Cleopatra* never once, I believe, go astray in this fashion, the F1 text of *Hamlet* presents us with the following grand total of fifteen instances:

1.5.135–6

(Q2) *Hora.* There's no offence my Lord.
     Ham. Yes by Saint Patrick but there is Horatio
(F1) *Hor.* There's no offence my Lord.
     Ham. Yes, by Saint Patricke, but there is *my Lord*

1.5.177

(Q2) or there be and if they might
(F1) or there be and if *there* might

2.2.52

(Q2) My newes shall be the fruite to that great feast.
(F1) My Newes shall be the *Newes* to that great Feast.

2.2.197

(Q2) I meane the matter that you reade my Lord
(F1) I meane the matter [that] you *meane*, my Lord

3.1.107–10

(Q2) ...you¹ should admit no discourse to your beautie.
     Oph. Could beauty my Lord haue better comerse
     Then with honestie?
(F1) ...your Honesty should admit no discourse to your Beautie.
     Ophe. Could Beautie my Lord, haue better Comerce then *your Honestie*?

3.2.68

(Q2) Since my deare soule was mistris of her choice
(F1) Since my deere Soule was Mistris of *my* choyse

---

¹ "You" is a misprint, probably through omission and miscorrection, of "your honestie", cf. pp. 142–3, and vol. II, p. 248.

3.2.184

(Q2) My operant powers their functions leaue to do
(F1) My operant Powers *my* Functions leaue to do

3.3.14

(Q2) That spirit, vpon whose weale depends and rests
(F1) That Spirit, vpon whose *spirit* depends and rests

3.4.11–12

(Q2) *Ger.* Come, come, you answere with an idle tongue.
    Ham. Goe, goe, you question with a wicked tongue.
(F1) *Qu.* Come, come, you answer with an idle tongue.
    Ham. Go, go, you question with *an idle* tongue.

3.4.87–8

(Q2) Since frost it selfe as actiuely doth burne,
    And reason pardons will.
(F1) Since Frost it selfe, as actiuely doth burne,
    As Reason panders Will.

4.5.12

(Q2) Indeede would make one thinke there might be thought
(F1) Indeed would make one thinke there *would* be thought

4.7.154–5

(Q2) Should haue a back or second that might hold
    If this did blast in proofe
(F1) Should haue a backe or second, that might hold,
    If this *should* blast in proofe

5.2.191–2

(Q2) there are no tongues els for's turne
(F1) there are no tongues else for's *tongue*

5.2.291

(Q2) *Ham.* Come on sir. *Laer.* Come my Lord
(F1) *Ham.* Come on sir. *Laer.* Come *on sir.*

5.2.40–1

(Q2) As loue betweene them like the palme might florish,
    As peace should still her wheaten garland weare
(F1) As loue betweene them, *as* the Palme *should* flourish,
    As Peace should still her wheaten Garland weare

The last example "stands a comma 'tween" the two classes of error we are now considering, since it shows us not only "as" repeated in the first line but also "should" anticipated from the line that follows.

Compositors may repeat words, but they are exceedingly unlikely to anticipate. Repetition is due to failure of memory. Their normal method of working is to pick up a certain number of words, generally not more than three or four, by the eye from the copy in front of them, and then turn to their stick and set them up in type, carrying the words as they do so in their heads. Now the head-carrying process involves an effort of memory, and memory plays tricks with the best of us. Thus it is easy enough to see how a word or phrase already memorised might get substituted for something else in the next group of words to be picked up by the compositor's eye. But how can compositors, not endowed with the gift of prophecy, anticipate words in their copy upon which their eye has not yet lighted? Such a feat is clearly impossible. And yet there are at least twenty-three instances of anticipation of this kind in the F1 text! It looks as if we are at last nearing a definite turning-point in our investigations.

But when we seem to sight the quarry we should be most on our guard. Anticipation is just possible for a compositor, if he has not mastered the head-carrying process and allows his eye to run ahead of the group of words he is committing to memory, though even so he will hardly do this except in one and the same line of his copy. Now, in Q2 we have a very poor compositor, as I have said, and though I think there is another and better explanation of them,[1] it is

    [1] *Vide* below, p. 143.

conceivable that anticipation by the eye may account for his making the following couple of misprints:

1.2.67

(F1) Not so my Lord, I am too much i'th'Sun
(Q2) Not so *much* my Lord, I am too much in the sonne.

2.2.566–7

(F1) a speech of some dosen or sixteene lines
(Q2) a speech of some dosen *lines*, or sixteene lines

The F1 text, on the other hand, gives us six instances of anticipation in the same line, as follows:

1.3.16

(Q2) The vertue of his will, but you must feare
(F1) The vertue of his *feare*: but you must feare

2.2.48

(Q2) As it hath vsd to doe, that I haue found
(F1) As I *haue* vs'd to doe: that I haue found

2.2.467

(Q2) one speech in't I chiefely loued
(F1) One *cheefe* Speech in it, I cheefely lou'd

3.4.44

(Q2) And sets a blister there, makes marriage vowes
(F1) And *makes* a blister there. Makes marriage vowes

4.5.89

(Q2) Feeds on this wonder, keepes himselfe in clowdes
(F1) *Keepes* on his wonder, keepes himselfe in clouds

5.2.109

(Q2) Nay good my Lord for my ease in good faith
(F1) Nay, *in good faith*, for mine ease in good faith

It is, of course, remotely conceivable that all six of the foregoing mistakes were made in Jaggard's office; but the fact that the F1 compositors seem otherwise competent enough and never, as far as I am aware, commit misprint

by anticipation in the seventeen Folio texts with which I
am familiar, renders it exceedingly improbable. Furthermore, while an incompetent compositor's eye might run
ahead for a word or two in the same line, instances of
anticipation of wider range than this are very rare indeed.[1]
Yet the agent who transmitted the F1 text, and whom we
are now driving into a corner, will anticipate words lines
ahead, or even at times words in quite different scenes.
Here are four examples in which he anticipates a word in
the following line:

1.3.117–18

(Q2) .Lends the tongue vowes, these blazes daughter
      Giuing more light then heate
(F1) *Giues* the tongue vowes: these blazes, Daughter,
      Giuing more light then heate

1.4.14–15

(Q2) But to my minde, though I am natiue heere
      And to the manner borne
(F1) *And* to my mind, though I am natiue heere,
      And to the manner borne

[1] I know of two examples beyond those here cited. One occurs
in Lavater's *Of Ghostes and Spirites walking by nyght*, trans. by
R. H. (Bynneman, 1572) which among the "Faultes escaped in the
Print" gives on p. 130, l. 31 "for beate, read chyde", the obvious cause
of the error being the word "beat" which is found two lines further
on in the text. The other was furnished me by Dr McKerrow, who
informs me that 2.2.623–6 of *Hamlet* in Pope's edition (1723) appears
as follows:

> "With most miraculous organ. I'll observe his looks,
> Play something like the murther of my father
> Before mine uncle. I'll observe his looks,
> I'll tent him to the quick."

Both examples are remarkably similar to those quoted from the F1
Hamlet, and may, I think, possibly be due to the same cause, viz.
transcription rather than press-composition.

2.1.14–15

(Q2) As thus, I know his father, and his friends,
         And in part him

(F1) *And* thus I know his father and his friends,
         And in part him

3.2.393–5

(Q2) *Ham.* Do you see yonder clowd that's almost in shape of
                a Camel?

         Pol. By'th masse and tis, like a Camell indeed.

(F1) *Ham.* Do you see *that* Clowd? that's almost in shape *like*
                a Camell.

         Pol. By'th'Misse, and it's like a Camell indeed

This last instance, it will be noticed, is a double one and
illustrates anticipation both within and without the line.

Of words anticipated two or more lines ahead there are
six examples, some of them explaining one or two of those
vulgarisations noted above. It is unnecessary to quote the
passages at length; the true reading from Q2, followed by
the F1 variant with the line or half-line from which the
anticipated word is borrowed, should suffice to show the
reader how the land lies.

I.I

150 (Q2) The Cock that is the trumpet to the morne
         (F1) The Cocke that is the Trumpet to the *day*
         ....
152   Awake the God of *Day*

I.I

161 (Q2) And then they say no spirit dare sturre abraode
         (F1) And then (they say) no Spirit can *walke* abroad
         ....
167   *Walkes* o're the dew of yon high Easterne Hill

I.2

82 (Q2) Together with all formes, moodes, chapes of griefe
         (F1) Together with all Formes, Moods, *shewes* of Griefe
         ....
85   But I haue that Within, which passeth *show*

2.2

529 (Q2)   With Bison rehume, a clout vppon that head
(F1)   With Bisson Rheume: A clout *about* that head
....
531   *About* her lanke and all ore-teamed Loines

2.2

579 (Q2)   Could force his soule so to his owne conceit
(F1)   Could force his soule so to his *whole conceit*
....
582   A broken voyce, and his *whole* Function suiting
           With Formes, to his *Conceit*

3.2

374–5 (Q2)   it wil discourse most eloquent musique
(F1)   it will discourse most *excellent Musicke*
....
384   there is much *Musicke, excellent* Voice, in this little
           Organe

In the last two examples Shakespeare's repetition of a word has assisted the process of anticipation. It is clear, for instance, that the person, or one of the persons, responsible for the F1 text, when he came to the dialogue between Hamlet and Guildenstern concerning the recorders, had already the words "music" and "excellent" closely associated together in his head, so that the association influenced his text nine lines before the two words actually occur in conjunction. Similarly, in the Hecuba soliloquy, the fact that the words "whole" and "conceit" are found in close proximity in ll. 582–3 is the reason why we find "whole conceit" in place of "own conceit" three lines earlier.

And if this seem far-fetched in more senses than one to any of my readers, let them consider even remoter connections of the same kind. Fortinbras is a character who has less than twenty-five lines to speak on the stage, and he appears twice only: once in 4.4 and again at the end of the play. Somehow the words of 5.2 have in F1 corrupted what he has to say in 4.4. The passage in question runs thus in Q2:

> Tell him, that by his lycence Fortinbrasse
> Craues the conueyance of a promisd march
> Ouer his kingdome.

Fortinbras speaks politely; after all that has happened at the beginning of the play, he is a suspect character in Denmark; he "craues" therefore. F1, however, makes him talk in a more peremptory vein:

> Tell him that by his license, Fortinbras
> *Claimes* the conueyance of a promis'd March
> Ouer his Kingdome.

It might be thought that the change is just one of those little chance substitutions of which the F1 *Hamlet* is full. But it is something more; for it is linked with two lines which belong to Fortinbras at 5.2.400–1:

> I haue some rights, of memory in this *kingdome*,
> Which now to *clame* my vantage doth inuite me.

Once again the repetition of a word by Shakespeare, the word "kingdom", has acted like a sort of memory-hook. "Kingdom" and "claim" have become associated, and so when "kingdom" occurs in an earlier speech in another scene by the same character, "claims" asserts itself and thrusts the more polite "craves" aside.

It is now clear that at the back of the F1 *Hamlet* there lies an active memory. And once this is realised, other verbal substitutions in that text find a natural and easy explanation. Take, for example, the error of "Satyricall slaue" (F1) for "satericall rogue" (Q2) at 2.2.198. This is accounted for by:

> O what a rogue and pesant slaue am I

of 2.2.576, where the conjunction of "rogue" and "slaue" has led to the interchange of the two words in the earlier passage. Again, the change from "barckt" to "bak'd"

(1.5.71), which looks like a case of omitted letters, may quite possibly be due to "crust" in the next line.[1] Or yet again, when at 4.3.65 Claudius speaks of the sealed orders which are to accompany Hamlet to England, he says, according to Q2:

> Our soueraigne processe, which imports at full
> By Letters congruing to that effect
> The present death of Hamlet.

But F1 prints "coniuring" for "congruing", and Dowden follows, on the ground that "this word, rather than the Q2 'congruing' corresponds with the 'earnest conjuration' of the document, described by Hamlet in 5.2.38". The observation is acute; yet knowing what we now know about the F1 text, we can see that the reason Dowden advances for preferring it here is really the explanation of how "coniuring" came to be substituted for "congruing". In other words, the two passages concerning the "grand commission" of Rosencrantz and Guildenstern have become mixed up in the memory of the transmitter, so that the language of the one has affected that of the other.

Human memory is a queer thing, and when misunderstanding lends it aid, it may produce strange results in a dramatic text. For "the proude mans contumely" (Q2) of Hamlet's most famous soliloquy, F1 gives us "the poore mans Contumely". The root cause of the error is probably sheer misunderstanding of the word "contumely"; yet I strongly suspect that

> ...the Spurnes
> That patient merit of the vnworthy takes,

a few lines further on, has something to do with it. Again, the change at 3.1.149 from "God hath giuen you one face" (Q2) to "God has giuen you one pace" (F1) was probably suggested by "you jig, you amble" at l. 150. The most

---

[1] Cf. p. 150.

interesting case of this kind of blended anticipation and misconception is to be found at 2.1.111, where Q2 prints:

> I am sorry, that with better heede and iudgement
> I had not coted him,

and F1:

> I am sorrie that with better *speed* and iudgement
> I had not quoted him.

How has "heede" been transformed into "speed"? In spite of the fact that the words rhyme, no *ductus litterarum* will help us here. The clue, I believe, is the word "coted", or "quoted" as F1 spells it. This word had two meanings, to which in the time of Shakespeare both spellings were appropriate, viz. (i) quoted, cited, or noted—the sense Polonius intends in the passage before us; and (ii) outstripped, a technical word used in the coursing of the hare, and occurring elsewhere in *Hamlet*, to wit at 2.2.330, where Rosencrantz, speaking of his passing the players on his journey to Elsinore with Guildenstern, says "we coted them on the way". Whether the man we are catching glimpses of behind the F1 text was influenced by a memory of Rosencrantz's words when transmitting those of Polonius, I do not venture to speculate; but I am very sure that his alteration of "heede" to "speed" was due to the fact that he set the wrong construction upon "coted". In other words, he knew the passage as a whole before he set to work transmitting it, placed an incorrect interpretation upon it, and altered a word, consciously or unconsciously, to suit this interpretation.

Finally, if we have to reckon upon an active memory in taking stock of the F1 *Hamlet*, we should expect to find it casting backwards as well as forwards; in other words, we should look out for reminiscence as well as anticipation. Strange to say, while we have been able to bring to light quite a large number of examples of the latter, reminiscence more remote than the fifteen instances of immediate repetition noted above[1] seem to be far less frequent. There are, however, some half-dozen F1 variants which I should attribute to this cause. The first three are simple enough. The earliest occurs at 1.3.120 and gives us the variants:

(Q2) You must not take for fire, from this time
(F1) You must not take for fire. For[2] this time Daughter,

where all modern editors have followed Q2 and where it is clear that the intrusive "Daughter" is simply a careless repetition of the last word in l. 117 above,

Giues the tongue vowes: these blazes, Daughter.

Next at 1.5.162 we have the variants:

(Q2) can'st worke it'h earth so fast
(F1) can'st worke i'th' ground so fast?

where the F1 "ground" is probably a recollection from "Shift our ground" half a dozen lines before. Again, at 2.1.55 F1 makes Polonius say

He closes with you thus. I know the Gentleman,

where the words "with you", which, as both metre and the Q2 text demonstrate, have been added to the line, are patently a recollection from l. 45 above:[3]

He closes with you in this consequence.

The fourth example is at once more complicated and more interesting. At the opening of 3.1 the King asks his spies, Rosencrantz and Guildenstern, according to Q2:

An can you by no drift of conference
Get from him why he puts on this confusion,

---

[1] *Vide* pp. 52–4.
[2] F1 misprint, repeating the "for" before "fire".
[3] It is interesting to observe that the corresponding words in Q1 are "he closeth with him thus". This may be just coincidence; on the other hand it may indicate that the F1 error is due to the transcriber's memory of what he had heard on the stage. Cf. below, p. 142.

and the first line of this appears in F1 as:

> And can you by no drift of *circumstance*,

a reading which all modern editors have adopted without giving their reasons. Yet the Q2 "drift of conference", which means "leading questions" or "cunning conversation", offers what is assuredly a much easier and pithier expression. As for the F1 reading, that arises, unless I am very much mistaken, from memories of another reference to spying earlier in the play, this time in the mouth of Polonius, who at 2.1.7–11 enjoins Reynaldo as follows:

> Enquire me first what Danskers are in Parris,
> And how, and who, what meanes, and where they keepe,
> What companie, at what expense, and finding
> By this *encompasment*, and *drift of question*
> That they doe know my sonne....

An unconscious recollection of "encompasment and drift of question" perhaps reinforced by Hamlet's

> And so without more circumstance at all,

at 1.5.127, is quite enough, in the light of the rest of the evidence, to account for "drift of circumstance". Two other examples, which come from 5.1.198 and 5.2.263, it will be more convenient to take later.[1]

Half a dozen pages ago we were discussing the tricks which the memory of compositors might play in the process of setting up a text in type. We have travelled a long way from that. The memory of compositors concerns the small groups of words which their eye picks up one after another from the copy before them. The memory we have just been studying is one that embraces the whole of *Hamlet*. It is not a "good memory", for it frequently leads its possessor astray. But it is certainly a vigorous memory, seeing that it as frequently interferes with the work he has in hand. Above all it is a comprehensive memory; it brings together words

[1] *Vide* vol. II, pp. 256, 257.

connected with similar trains of thought from different passages, references to the same topics from different scenes, speeches by the same character from different acts. The reader will be already aware of the direction in which the evidence has been driving us. The agent responsible for the preparation of the F1 *Hamlet* must have been a copyist possessed of a pretty thorough knowledge of the play, upon which he relied over-much in the preparation of his transcript. He had, we must suppose, a good text of some kind before him as he worked—for it would be absurd to imagine that he wrote the whole play out from memory—but confident of his acquaintance with the various parts, he often allowed his pen to run straight on without checking what he wrote with that from which he was copying. This confidence, indeed, was his undoing, or rather the undoing of the F1 version. For all, or almost all, the gross imperfections of that text, which have been the theme of this present section—the mistakes in the use of the verb, the confusion between plural and singular in the noun, the careless omission of words and phrases, the misapprehension of Shakespeare's language, the debasement of his diction and his metre, as well as the slovenly verbal repetitions and anticipations which in the end revealed his existence to us —must be set down to his account. And all may be explained by the irresponsible self-confidence with which he set about his task. The transcription of 3500 lines is a heavy piece of work, and the perpetual reference to the document to be transcribed a tiresome necessity in the making of any copy. How powerful then would be the temptation for a copyist who thought he knew his *Hamlet*, to trust to that knowledge and ease his labour by so trusting!

What kind of man was this transcriber? For what purpose did he make his copy? And what was the text he used in making it? The first of these questions admits of only one answer. He was a player or theatrical scrivener thoroughly familiar with the play upon the stage, and (since the whole

Folio bears the endorsement of Heminge and Condell) he must assuredly have belonged to their company and to the Globe theatre. As for his purpose in transcribing the text, that too is not difficult to guess. He was certainly not making his copy for stage-performance; as we have seen, the F1 text is so bad that it cannot possibly have served as prompt-book in any reputable theatre. Moreover, the very carelessness with which he went to work is an indication that he knew his transcription would never be brought to the test of theatrical representation, since that would at once have exposed his inattentive dealing with the original. On the other hand, what likelihood was there of his being brought to account for slovenliness in a text two-thirds of the way through a volume embracing the whole of Shakespeare's plays? Even three centuries of editors have left him undetected. In a word, the obvious purpose of the transcript was to serve as copy for Jaggard's printers in 1623; that is to say, the copyist was one of Heminge and Condell's staff told off to prepare the material for F1. It is a disconcerting notion, since it casts a sinister light upon the "editorial" methods employed in the production of that famous corpus; but I do not see that we have any alternative. Incidentally, too, it goes far to ease the textual situation for editors; since it relieves the prompt-book and performance at the Globe of any responsibility for the mass of corruption in the F1 *Hamlet*, and explains further how words which, on the combined evidence of Q1 and Q2, were certainly spoken on the Globe stage, came to be altered later for the worse.

And what of the text from which the transcript was made? The answer to that too is simple enough. While the transcript itself can never have been used as a prompt-book, all the evidence brought forward in section III of this chapter goes to prove a close connection between the F1 text and the prompt-book in use at the Globe. In other words, the transcript was prepared by a Globe copyist from the prompt-book in that theatre. As for the theory, glanced at on pp. 17–8, 40, that the F1 text might in some way be derived from the printed quarto of 1605, we can now see it to be quite untenable. A printed book cannot possibly have been used as Jaggard's copy for *Hamlet*, since that copy is demonstrably a transcript. Nor is it any more conceivable that a quarto served as the prompt-book and that the transcriber himself therefore copied from such a specimen. If the prompt-book were already in print, why should he go to the trouble of copying it out for the purpose of reprinting it? Why did he not procure a second copy of the quarto, and by collating it with the copy in use at the Globe bring it into line with the authoritative prompt-book? It is clear that the 1605 *Hamlet* or its reprints, the Smethwick quartos, do not at any point come into the pedigree of the F1 text. And it is not at all difficult to understand why the players would have nothing to do with that version. We shall discover in our next chapter that it is one of the worst printed of Shakespearian texts. It teems with misprints of all kinds; its verbal omissions amount to 96, and its omitted lines and half-lines to 111. Picture the condition of a specimen of Q2, with all its stage-directions rewritten, its omissions filled up, its misprints corrected, and the multifarious other interlinear and marginal alterations and additions required to bring it into the hypothetical state of the Globe prompt-book. Is it really conceivable that such an impossibly confused and difficult "book" can ever have served as prompt-copy for the leading company in London?

The original Globe prompt-book at the beginning of the seventeenth century was a transcript from Shakespeare's manuscript, and the copy used by Jaggard's printers in 1623 was a transcript of that transcript. This is as certain as anything can be in a realm of enquiry which must always, in the nature of things, remain a realm of conjecture. Yet, even so, it needs qualification. For it is conceivable that the original prompt-book of a popular play like *Hamlet* may have been thumbed to pieces in the twenty years between its transcription in 1601 and the preparation of the copy for Jaggard. And this would mean that we must allow for a third transcript in the genealogy of transmission.

§ V. THE TWO SCRIBES OF THE FOLIO TEXT

Two copyists at least, then, stand between Shakespeare's original *Hamlet* and the compositors of the text of 1623; one of them the transcriber whose iniquities have been the subject of the previous section, and the other the more accomplished person responsible, directly or indirectly, for the cuts and stage directions discussed in § III. It will be convenient to give them names. The former, a mere copyist, we may call Scribe C; and the latter, who is closely associated with the Globe prompt-book, may be designated Scribe P. Can we distinguish the one from the other at any given point in F1? Can we, that is to say, classify the errors in that production under three different heads: the compositor's, Scribe C's and Scribe P's? It is obvious that any such clear-cut distinction is quite out of the question, since all we know about Scribe P is what we can glean from the transcription of his text by Scribe C, itself only visible through the type of Jaggard's workmen. Nor fortunately is it a matter of any great moment for an editor. I have accordingly in Appendix C drawn up a list of F1 readings rejected by the Cambridge editors of 1866, and have roughly classified them on the lines already set forth on pp. 44–5. But except for § (*b*) of this Appendix, which I have been bold enough to label "Compositors' Slips", I have not attempted to assign the errors to their respective agents of corruption. We can, for instance, feel pretty certain that the curious misprints in *r* quoted on p. 45 were due to one or other of the scribes; but who can say which? The list of Abnormal Spellings again, while including a number which may be Shake-spearian,[1] reveals others like "gidge" (jig), "pick haxe" (pick-axe), for which there are no parallels in the good quartos, together with a strong propensity, quite unlike anything we know of Shakespeare, for spellings in "i" such as "secricie", "rapsidie", "cerimony", "ventiges", and in "c" such as "rouce" (rouse), "bace" (base), "rac'd" (raz'd). But whether these spellings belonged to Scribe P or Scribe C it is impossible to determine. On the other hand, while it is tempting to attribute most of what I have called "Errors possibly due to Misreading" to Scribe P working directly from Shakespeare's autograph, since they tally on the whole with the kind of errors we find in Q2 and in other texts probably printed from Shakespearian manuscripts, we have no certainty of this, inasmuch as such errors are common enough in books of the period and may therefore be due to either of the other two agents of corruption.

Yet we can never be too curious concerning Shake-spearian texts. There are indisputable departures from the author's intention in the F1 *Hamlet* which we may, I think, with fair probability allocate to one or other of the two scribes; and we are enabled to do this in the main because the bad quarto has preserved for us many of the readings actually spoken on the stage shortly after the prompt-book was first made out.

(*a*) Emendations and errors attributable to Scribe P

We have assumed in § III that the bulk of the stage-directions, assignment of speeches, and cuts which dis-tinguish F1 from Q2 are the work of Scribe P, and we

---

[1] "aygre" (1.4.2; 1.5.69) is an interesting example, being closely connected with Fr. *aigre* (*vide* Greg, *Emendation*, p. 64; *Aspects*, p. 192).

were encouraged in this assumption not only by the general probabilities of the situation but also by the fact that in almost every case where we can check these matters with Q1, the latter agrees with F1.

There are, too, similarities in the arrangement of speeches, of which the following will serve as an example. At 1.5.157–61, Q2 gives us

> Come hether Gentlemen
> And lay your hands againe vpon my sword,
> Sweare by my sword
> Neuer to speake of this that you haue heard.
> *Ghost.* Sweare by his sword.

The comma after "sword" in l. 158 allows for a pause while Hamlet presents the hilt of his weapon, and Horatio and Marcellus step forward to lay their hands upon it. Subject to this natural interpretation the Q2 text seems entirely unexceptionable.[1] But the thrice repeated "sword" apparently disturbed Scribe P, and F1 accordingly prints the passage thus:

> Come hither Gentlemen,
> And lay your hands againe vpon my sword,
> Neuer to speake of this that you haue heard:
> Sweare by my Sword.
> *Gho.* Sweare.

And that we owe the rearrangement to Scribe P and not to his successor is, I think, proved by Q1, which offers us a report of the F1 version, as follows:

> Come hither Gentlemen, and lay your handes
> Againe vpon this sword, neuer to speake
> Of that which you haue seene, sweare by my sword.
> *Ghost.* Sweare.

As it happens, a close parallel with the foregoing occurs a

---

[1] But cf. Greg, *Emendation*, p. 57; *Aspects*, p. 184.

few lines farther on at 1.5.179–82, as will be evident from quotation of the three texts:

(Q2)   ...this doe sweare,
  So grace and mercy at your most neede helpe you.
  Ghost. Sweare.

(F1)   ...this not to doe:
  So grace and mercy at your most neede helpe you
  Sweare.
  Ghost. Sweare.

(Q1) This not to doe, so grace, and mercie
  At your most need helpe you, sweare.
  Ghost. sweare.

These variants imply not merely linear rearrangement, but also deliberate alteration of the text, and remind us that our Scribe P in straightening out the tangles and re-shaping the stage-business, as we have seen him doing in § III, was prepared to alter the text proper, that is the actual words of the dialogue, without any hesitation when it suited his purposes. He deals with cruxes by cutting out the passages which contain them; he tidies up the loose ends in the Gonzago play; he adds a word here or omits a word there when his revised stage-directions make such changes necessary. Furthermore, he edits Shakespeare. He strikes out the superfluous words "Eyther none" which, as is clear from Q2, were accidentally left standing at the beginning of 3.2.178 but have disappeared in F1. Similarly the Q2 reading at 2.2.73:

Giues him threescore thousand crownes in anuall fee,

which shows us Shakespeare naming a sum of money, in the hurry or absorption of composition, too large for the limits of blank-verse, offered no difficulty to Scribe P, for the corresponding line in F1 and Q1:

Giues him three thousand Crownes in Annuall Fee,

proves that he solved it with a single stroke of the pen.

But the pen might be more injurious in its operation. It

is not surprising that he should take a high line with anything he cannot read or understand; and there are, I think, a fair number of F1 variants which should be set down to his emending hand. We may, for instance, unless I am much mistaken, watch him at work in a passage (2.2.614–16) from the Hecuba soliloquy which runs thus in the two main versions:

(Q2)   Must like a whore vnpacke my hart with words,
          And fall a cursing like a very drabbe; a stallyon, fie vppont,
          foh.

(F1)   Must (like a Whore) vnpacke my heart with words,
          And fall a Cursing like a very Drab,
          A Scullion? Fye vpon't: Foh.

All editors since Pope and Jennens have read "scullion" with F1, and can cite "scalion", an obvious misprint of the same word, from Q1 in support. Nevertheless, there can be no doubt that "stallyon" was the word Shakespeare wrote, since its seventeenth-century connotation of a "male whore"[1] fits in exactly with the "whore" and "drab" immediately before. The same story is repeated in a very different connection at 4.7.178, which in the three texts gives us these variants:

> (Q2)   she chaunted snatches of old laudes
> (F1)   she chaunted snatches of old tunes
> (Q1)   Chaunting olde sundry tunes,

the last being of course simply a report of the F1 version. All modern editors have accepted the F1 emendation, and by so doing have sacrificed a beautiful reading. For "laudes" means hymns of praise and is apparently a reference to the *laude* or vernacular hymns which were first heard of in Italy at the end of the thirteenth century, were sung by wandering bands or guilds of singers called *laudesi*, and were still very popular at the end of the fifteenth. Whether they were also the fashion in England or how

---

[1] Cf. *N.E.D.* "Stallion" 2*b* and 3.

Shakespeare came to know of them is not clear. But it can hardly be questioned that his use of the word here was intended to show the drowning Ophelia crowned with flowers and singing hymns of praise to God for the wonders of creation.[1]

Yet another instance, taken from 4.2.18–20, may perhaps be a case of mistranscription rather than emendation. In any event the alteration evidently passed into the prompt-book and on to the stage, as is shown by the Q1 reading. Hamlet, speaking of the spongy officers of the King, remarks according to the three texts:

(Q2) he keepes them like an apple in the corner of his iaw, first mouth'd to be last swallowed

(F1) He keepes them like an Ape in the corner of his iaw, first mouth'd to be last swallowed

(Q1) For hee doth keep you as an Ape doth nuttes, In the corner of his Iaw, first mouthes you, Then swallows you.

Once again, though all the editors follow F1, the Q2 offers an excellent reading, and one that the

Youths that thunder at a playhouse, and fight for bitten apples[2]

would have fully appreciated. For some reason, however, Scribe P altered "apple" to "ape", and the reading of the bad quarto gives us perhaps the kind of sense that Burbadge put upon it, though there is little enough that is sponge-like in nuts! Two further examples of less importance may be added. In both the Q2 reading is unimpeachable, and in both all editors have succumbed to the agreement between F1 and Q1. In the first, from 2.2.406–7—

(Q2) a Monday morning, t'was then indeede

(F1) for a Monday morning 'twas so indeed

(Q1) a monday last, t'was so indeede—

[1] I am indebted for the information above to *Old Picture Books* (pp. 15–22) by Dr A. W. Pollard. It is possible that Shakespeare had in mind also Psalms cxlviii–cl which are sung at the service of Lauds.

[2] *Hen. VIII*, 5.4.63–4.

the word "then" is obviously more in keeping with the context than "so". And in the second, from 2.2.524,

(Q2) But who, a woe, had seene the mobled Queene
(F1) But who, O who, had seen the mobled[1] Queen
(Q1) But who, O who had seene the mobled Queene—

the "ah, woe!" of the good quarto is to my mind unquestionably better than the mere repetition of the other texts.

There are no doubt other emendations in F1, for which Q1 offers no parallel and therefore no control, but which nevertheless belong to Scribe P and the original prompt-book. And I think we shall generally be justified in ascribing to his hand any change that clearly represents an attempt to make sense of a word which a nonsensical variant in Q2 suggests was difficult to read in Shakespeare's manuscript. Most of these will be considered later, when we have made a thorough examination of Q2 and of its production by the printers in 1605, seeing that until we know exactly what we are dealing with in that text, we cannot use it with confidence as a touchstone for F1 readings. Three fairly obvious emendations of the kind may, however, be glanced at here; the first a strikingly happy one.

One of Hamlet's speeches (3.4.48–51) in the bedroom scene with his mother concludes in the text of 1605 with this crux:

> heauens face dooes glowe
> Ore this solidity and compound masse
> With heated visage, as against the doome
> Is thought sick at the act.

Whether through crowding at the foot of a page, or because Shakespeare's handwriting was peculiarly difficult at this point, something—not I believe much—has gone wrong with the text, though what exactly it was we shall enquire later. Enough that his copy baffled the Q2 com-

---

[1] F1 misprints this word "inobled".

positor at this point, and that those responsible for the prompt-book were equally baffled. For the passage appears in F1 as follows:

> Heauens face doth glow,
> Yea this solidity and compound masse,
> With tristfull visage as against the doome,
> Is thought-sicke at the act.

The changes are very skilful. In particular, the substitution of "tristfull" for "heated" shows a command of poetic diction so persuasive, that most modern editors have swallowed the emendation whole and followed the F1 text. Knowing, however, what we now know about the two texts, we have only to compare it with the Q2 reading to see that it cannot be what Shakespeare originally wrote. And yet it seems too intelligent altogether for Scribe C. The example is an instructive one; and I shall return to it.[1]

Nor does it stand alone. It is closely paralleled by the variant readings at 3.3.5–7, already quoted in the first chapter, in which the F1 "Lunacies" is now seen to be a later emendation of some illegible word in Shakespeare's handwriting which the Q2 compositor set up as "browes". It is paralleled also at 2.2.137, where Q2 reads

> Or giuen my hart a working mute and dumbe,

and F1

> Or giuen my heart a winking, mute and dumbe,

which, as usual, all editors I believe since Pope have followed. Yet here the F1 variant is a case of sheer misunderstanding. For there can be no doubt at all, despite the editors, that "working" was the word Shakespeare intended. He uses it again in *Love's Labour's Lost* ("the working of the heart", 4.1.33), *Sonnet* 93 ("Whate'er thy thoughts or thy heart's workings be"), and 1 *Henry VI* ("sick with working of my thoughts", 5.5.86); examples which show

[1] *Vide* pp. 166–9.

that the word was a regular expression with him for mental operation of any kind. Thus to give one's "heart a working mute and dumb" means very much what to "play the desk or table-book" means in the previous line, namely, to store up impressions or thoughts without saying anything about them. Not understanding this, the scribe has emended to "winking", i.e. sleep, which indeed from its graphical similarity with "working" he may have supposed that Shakespeare actually wrote. The emendation will not do, if for no other reason than that "mute and dumb" goes very awkwardly with it; but it is distinctly ingenious, and belongs to the same order of intelligence as that which read "Lunacies" for "browes" at 3.3.7.

There is nothing, I have said, in Q1 to compare with the three foregoing emendations. But we have not yet exhausted the possibilities of Q1 as an independent touchstone. Scribe P or his agent was a far more careful transcriber than Scribe C, but he had his moments of aberration, which have left their traces in both the F1 and Q1 texts. Occasionally, for instance, he omitted small words, as is clear from the following parallels:

1.5.29

(Q2) Hast me to know't, that I with wings as swift
(F1) Hast, hast me to know it, That with wings as swift
(Q1) Haste me to knowe it, that with wings as swift

4.5.37

(Q2) Larded all with sweet flowers
(F1) Larded with sweet flowers
(Q1) Larded with sweete flowers

4.5.195

(Q2) His beard was as white as snow
(F1) His Beard as white as Snow
(Q1) His beard as white as snowe.

In the second of these three examples, F1 and Q1 are

followed by all editors, and the change was perhaps deliberately made in order to restore the metre; nevertheless, I am convinced that the Quarto of 1605 preserves Shakespeare's intention, which was to give Ophelia unmetrical lines in order to emphasise her disordered utterance.[1]

Among the following coincidences between F1 and Q1 some no doubt are accidental, but they can hardly all be so.

Q2	F1	Q1
	1.5.58	
morning ayre	Mornings Ayre	As F1
	1.5.151	
Come on, you heare	Come one you here	come you here,
	2.1.99	
without theyr helps	without their helpe	As F1
	2.2.205	
shall growe old	should be old	shalbe olde
	2.2.333	
haue tribute on me	haue Tribute of mee	As F1
	2.2.462	
were no sallets	was no Sallets	As F1
	2.2.617	
About my braines	About my Braine	As F1
	3.2.240	
doth protest too much	protests to much	protests too much

Here also are a couple of inversions,[2] which may be accidentally coincident, or may indeed be errors in Q2:

3.2.105

(Q2) That did I my Lord
(F1) That I did my Lord
(Q1) That I did my L:

[1] Cf. vol. II, pp. 292–3.   [2] Cf. vol. II, 262.

5.1.285

(Q2) Yet haue I in me something
(F1) Yet haue I something in me
(Q1) For there is something in me.

Finally there are two instances in which the F1 and Q1 coincident variants are clearly actor's additions, and will therefore be more conveniently considered in the section that follows.

(b) Burbadge's additions to his part

Dowden noted, in the passage already quoted[1] from his introduction to the Arden *Hamlet*, as a characteristic of the F1 text that "Some actors' additions are introduced, such as the unhappy 'O, o, o, o' of the dying Hamlet, following his words 'The rest is silence'"; and he is undoubtedly correct. On p. 349 (Appendix C (d) iv), under the head "Added words", will be found a list of words in F1 which Aldis Wright regarded as superfluous and therefore omitted from *The Cambridge Shakespeare*. Of these twenty-four instances, no less than sixteen are just the sort of little ejaculatory words or phrases which a player in the excitement of performance would be likely to add to his lines, as will be evident when the passages are set out, with the Q2 equivalents in brackets:

1.2.132 O God, O God (ô God, God)
  135 Oh fie, fie (ah fie)
  243 I warrant you (I warn't)
1.4. 45 Oh, oh, answer me (ô answere mee)
1.5. 29 Hast, hast me to know it (Hast me to know't)
1.5.104 yes, yes, by Heauen (yes by heauen)
       (Q1) 'Yes, yes, by heauen'
  107 My Tables, my Tables (My tables)

      [1] *Vide* p. 13.

2.2. 85 This businesse is very well ended (This busines is well
             ended)
     174 Excellent, excellent well (Excellent well)
     406 for a Monday morning (a Monday morning)
     608 a Bawdy villaine (baudy villaine)
     611 I sure, this is most braue (this is most braue)
3.1. 76 these Fardles (fardels)
3.2. 7 the Whirle-winde (whirlwind)
4.3. 42 this deed of thine, for thine (this deede for thine)
4.7.165 they'l follow (they follow).

Further, the remarkable fact that thirteen out of the sixteen
belong to Hamlet's part suggests that the actor in Shakespeare's company most prone to such additions was the
great Burbadge himself. Such a supposition would explain
the preposterous "O, o, o, o" after "The rest is silence".
Scribe C, as we have seen, had vivid memories of *Hamlet*
on the stage, and was perhaps a fond admirer of the greatest
actor of the age. If so, it would be easy to understand how
he came to add to his text the dying groans—no doubt very
effective—of his hero, that he might "lose no drop of the
immortal man".[1]

We get similar additions in other dramatic texts of the
period. Dr Greg, for example, has discovered a number in
the 1594 quarto of Greene's *Orlando Furioso*, which he
describes as "connective insertions" and explains as actors'
tricks of speech transmitted by some scribe familiar with
the play on the stage, and reconstructing the text from
memory.[2] In the same way they are to be found in the bad
quartos of Shakespeare, which are likewise in the main
probably reported versions of what the pirate heard in the

---

[1] The explanation is supported by a similar "O, o, o, o" which
appears as the final utterance of Lear in the "Pied Bull" quarto of
King Lear, a text that on Dr Greg's showing is certainly based upon
a report of stage-performance; *vide The Function of Bibliography in
Literary Criticism*, by W. W. Greg (*Neophilologus*, XVIII, Amsterdam).
[2] W. W. Greg, *Two Elizabethan Stage Abridgements*, pp. 316–18.

theatre. But, unless I am mistaken, they also occur in F1 texts[1] other than *Hamlet*, to say nothing of Elizabethan plays outside the Shakespearian canon; and their presence in such good texts has generally, I think, been accounted for as players' tricks of speech creeping into the prompt-book or into actors' parts. This explanation has always puzzled me. How did such trivial additions come to be inserted in a prompt-book? Or, a more pertinent question perhaps, why should they be inserted therein? Even if the prompter noticed that a player had the trick of ejaculating "Oh!" occasionally without author's warrant, why should he go out of his way to write up such tricks? As long as the player in question continued to act the part, he would need no prompting in his little ejaculations; and if another player took the part over, there seems no point in obliging him to take over his predecessor's corruptions as well. But if we are dealing, not with the original prompt-book, but with a playhouse transcript from it of the kind we have found in the F1 *Hamlet*, nothing is more natural than that the transcriber should accidentally, or even at times deliberately (as perhaps in the case of the "O, o, o, o" enormity), transfer the tricks of the actors to his copy. He was inclined to rely in *Hamlet* on his memory, the memory of what he had heard on the stage. His text therefore, though technically a transcription, partakes to some extent of the character of a reported version. In a word, the condition and provenance of the F1 *Hamlet* suggests that any other F1 text, or for that matter any dramatic text of the period whatever, apart from pirated or reported texts, may be suspected of being a transcript by some playhouse copyist when it contains "connective insertions".

But there is a further point about these additions in *Hamlet* which has recently attracted some attention. A number of them, a third at least, consist of repetitions or

[1] *Two Gent.* 3.2.71, 4.3.4, 13; *Meas.* 2.2.165, 2.4.153, 3.1.54 (notes in "New Shakespeare").

reiterations. Now Dr A. C. Bradley in his *Shakespearean
Tragedy*, accepting the *Globe* text of Clark and Wright
without question, notes that repetition of this kind is a
trick of Hamlet's in speaking.[1] It is only necessary to quote

(*Globe*) Indeed, indeed, sirs, but this troubles me.
      Very like, very like. Stay'd it long?
      Words, words, words.
      Except my life, except my life, except my life.
      I humbly thank you; well, well, well—

to show that his observation is just enough. And yet,
though these familiar reiterations almost seem to give us
the very sound of Hamlet's voice, they are puzzling directly
one begins to consider them from the textual point of view;
and a modern Dutch critic, Dr H. de Groot, has even gone
so far as to declare that Shakespeare never intended them
at all, that they are in fact mere interpolations on the part
of Burbadge.[2]

Prima facie, indeed, he seems to have all the facts on his
side, however much our sense of dramatic fitness may rebel
against his conclusion. In the first place, in three out of the
five instances just quoted the repetition is only found in F1,
Q2 simply giving us

      Indeede, Sirs but this troubles me.
      Very like, stayd it long?
      I humbly thanke you well.

In the second place, as we have seen, F1 has a tendency to
such repetitions, and certainly repeats words and phrases at
points where Shakespeare intended no such thing; for
example,

1.2.

132 (Q2) ô God, God	(F1) O God, O God.	
135 (Q2) ah fie,	(F1) Oh fie, fie	

---

[1] Bradley, *Shakespearean Tragedy*, pp. 148–9.
[2] H. de Groot, *Hamlet: its Textual History*, pp. 34–6; van Dam,
Text of Shakespeare's Hamlet, pp. 98–9, takes much the same line.

1.4.

45 (Q2) ô answere mee   (F1) Oh, oh, answer me.

1.5.

29 (Q2) Hast me to know't   (F1) Hast, hast me to know it
104 (Q2) yes, by heauen   (F1) yes, yes, by Heauen
107 (Q2) My tables   (F1) My Tables, my Tables

That the iterations are here non-Shakespearian is proved
by the fact that they disturb the metre; the last mentioned,
for instance, gives us the line

    My Tables, my Tables; meet it is I set it downe.

And in the third place, if Burbadge had the habit of reitera-
tion, we should expect to find examples in the reported
Quarto of 1603 which do not appear in the Folio. And
this is exactly what we do find, as the following instances
out of a number in Q1 will show:

1.2.

    184 O my father, my father, me thinks I see my father
    254 O your loues, your loues, as mine to you

1.5.

    40–1 O my prophetike soule, my vncle! my vncle!
    118 O wonderfull, wonderful.

Dr de Groot's case looks impregnable; and yet there
must be a flaw somewhere, if there is anything in Dr
Bradley's contention at all. How shall we find the concord
of this discord? We may find it, I think, by observing one
or two factors which Dr de Groot has overlooked. First
of all, the omission of words and phrases is, as we have
remarked more than once already, even more conspicuous
in the Q2 than in the F1 text. It follows therefore that the
absence of repetitions or iterations in Q2 which are to be

found in F1 is no evidence that Shakespeare did not intend them, seeing that they may simply have been omitted by the compositor in 1605. Further, if iteration which disturbs the metre is to be set down as non-Shakespearian, iteration which is necessary to the metrical or rhythmical structure of the verse (and, I would venture to add, of the prose also), ought by the same line of argument to be regarded as undoubtedly Shakespeare's. Thus we may reassure ourselves concerning "Indeed, indeed, sirs", "Very like, very like", "well, well, well", since despite the fact that the repetitions are missing in Q2 they are essential to the metre in all three instances. Dr Bradley is then perfectly right; such repetitions are characteristic of Hamlet, and were given him no doubt as an expression of his brooding temperament. On the other hand, the extra-metrical repetitions in the Hamlet part, as printed in F1 and Q1, suggest that Dr de Groot is equally correct in his theory that Burbadge had a trick of "damnable iteration" at emotional moments of the performance. And are not these two points of view reconcilable? Is it not quite natural that Burbadge should seize upon a striking feature in the rôle he had to play, and—actor-like—exaggerate it?

(c) Profanity in the Folio text

It will be convenient at this point to say something on the question of the treatment of oaths and expletives in the F1 text. In May 1606 the famous "Act to Restrain Abuses of Players" was passed, which imposed a penalty of £10 for profane or jesting use of sacred names upon the stage; and the following comparative table makes it clear that the Globe prompt-book of *Hamlet* was to some extent revised in accordance with this Act:

Table illustrating the use of profane expletives in F1 and Q2

	Q2	F1	Q1[1]
1.2.150	O God	O Heauen!	O God
195	For Gods loue	For Heauens loue	For Gods loue
1.5. 24	O God	Oh Heauen!	O God
2.1. 50	By the masse	*om.*	
76	i'th name of God	in the name of Heauen	
114	By heauen	It seemes	By heau'n
2.2.384	s'bloud	*om.*	
603	Hah, s'wounds	Ha? Why	Sure
3.2.386	s'bloud	Why	Zownds
395	By'th masse	By'th'Misse	
4.5.199	God a mercy	Gramercy	God a mercy
201	ô God	you Gods	O God, O God!
5.1.297	S'wounds shew	Come show	Shew
5.2.355	O god	O good	O fie

On the other hand, F1 reads "O God" three times (1.2.132; 2.2.260; 3.2.132), "Fore God" once (2.2.488), "Before my God" once (1.1.56), "For loue of God" once (5.1.296), "God-a-mercy" once (2.2.172), "Gods bodykins" once (2.2.554), "By gis" once (4.5.59), "Oh Heauens" twice (3.2.138; 4.5.159), and "By Heauen" seven times (1.1.49; 1.4.85; 1.5.104, 120, 122; 4.5.156; 5.2.354).

These facts and figures seem to point to very perfunctory revision, and this accords with what is found in other F1 texts. Such haphazard treatment of profanity has hitherto been "something of a puzzle", to use Sir Edmund Chambers' words.[2] It was the business of the Master of the Revels to see that the play-books observed the statute, which would mean in the case of *Hamlet*, for example, that he would either have looked through the prompt-copy and

---

[1] Q1 was of course published three years before the Act of 1606.

[2] *Vide William Shakespeare*, I, 238–42, for a lengthy discussion of the matter and cf. W. W. Greg, *Merry Wives of Windsor, 1602*, pp. xxxvi, liv–lvi.

purged it of oaths on the occasion of its first revival after
May 1606, or would have accepted the company's word
that they had themselves so purged it. But purging the
"book" would not necessarily prevent oaths upon the stage;
and until the strait-laced Sir Henry Herbert came to the
Revels Office in 1622, it was probably pretty safe for the
players to follow their old practice of free profanity in the
theatre itself, whatever the censor might do with the prompt-
copy. At any rate, this seems to offer the simplest explanation of the facts in the above table. For those facts do not
forbid us to suppose that the *Hamlet* prompt-book had been
thoroughly purged; all they necessarily imply is that following his usual practice, Scribe C occasionally substituted
the expletive actually uttered on the stage for the tamer
word on the paper before him. To be precise, if my theory
is correct, he followed his copy twelve times and his memory
eight; for, since none of the ejaculations with "heaven" in
them were counted as profane, the variant "It seemes"
for "By heauen" at 2.1.114 must have been just one of
those chance pieces of carelessness of which this transcript
is full.

Further, if such an explanation prove acceptable for the
haphazard treatment of profanity in the F1 *Hamlet*, is
it not at least conceivable that careless playhouse transcription, or at least careless collation with the prompt-book,
may be the solution of similar inconsistency in other F1
texts? For example, when editing *Love's Labour's Lost*
I noted that of the twenty-one instances of the word "God"
in the 1598 quarto, one only had been changed to "Ioue"
in the F1 text.[1] If the latter had been printed direct from
a copy of the quarto which had served as prompt-book in
the theatre, this single recognition of the statute would be
indeed remarkable. If, on the other hand, it was printed
from a copy of the quarto which had merely been "corrected" by some scribe from the prompt-book, whether

[1] *Vide Love's Labour's Lost* ("New Shakespeare"), p. 190.

printed quarto or transcript, all would be explained. For while such a scribe would make no special effort to remove technical profanities from the quarto he was preparing as copy for Jaggard, it is likely enough that among his "corrections" one or two changes of the kind would appear, as the prompt-book variants happened to catch his eye.

(d) Scribe C's hand in the stage-directions and act-divisions of the Folio

An examination of certain F1 stage-directions in § III led us to the conclusion that the 1623 text was based upon a prompt-book at the Globe Theatre. In other words, we ascribed those stage-directions to Scribe P. We must never forget, however, that we can only see Scribe P's work through Scribe C's transcript; and that this copyist, demonstrably careless in other particulars, was not likely always to transmit his predecessor's stage-directions with perfect accuracy, though, being himself a player, he may well have given greater heed to them than to Shakespeare's lines. That he almost certainly omitted a number we shall later find reason for supposing.[1] Here we may establish the fact of his interference in the matter by considering a passage in 3.2, where the F1 variant can only be explained, I think, on the hypothesis that he was deliberately tinkering with an entry. The illustration is the more interesting inasmuch as, though all editors have followed Q2, none seems to have understood Shakespeare's intention any more than did Scribe C who departed from it.

The Dumb-show over, Ophelia wonderingly enquires "What means this, my lord?", to which Hamlet replies "Marry, this is miching mallecho; it means mischief". "Belike this show imports the argument of the play?" she then conjectures; whereupon a player appears before the

[1] *Vide* vol. II, pp. 182 ff.

curtain of the inner-stage and a dialogue ensues, which may be printed in the form that Q2 gives it.

Enter Prologue.

Ham. We shall know by this fellow,
The Players cannot keepe [counsel],[1] they'le tell all.
Oph. Will a tell vs what this show meant?
Ham. I, or any show that you will show him, be not you asham'd to show, heele not shame to tell you what it meanes.
Oph. You are naught, you are naught, Ile mark the play.
Prologue. For vs and for our Tragedie,
Heere stooping to your clemencie,
We begge your hearing patiently.
Ham. Is this a Prologue, or the posie of a ring?

When we turn to F1 we find *Enter Prologue* printed immediately before the words of the "posy" prologue itself, and it is clear that one of the agents responsible for that text made the change without perceiving that the intervening dialogue between Hamlet and Ophelia has reference to the entry. Indeed, so insensible was he of the fact that he even went to the trouble of rewriting the dialogue in the following manner:

Ham. We shall know by these Fellowes: the Players cannot keepe counsell, they'l tell all.
Ophe. Will they tell vs what this shew meant?
Ham. I, or any shew that you'l shew him. Bee not you asham'd to shew, hee'l not shame to tell you what it meanes.
Ophe. You are naught, you are naught, Ile marke the Play.

Enter Prologue.

He is a slap-dash person, it will be observed; he alters "this fellow" to "these Fellowes" and "a" to "they", but the "him" and "hee'l" in Hamlet's second speech have escaped his notice. It seems to me inconceivable that Scribe P, the competent prompter as we have seen him to be, could have been guilty of this careless piece of adaptation, or that even

[1] Q2 omits this word.

if he were the textual inconsistency could have survived in the prompt-book for over twenty years. We need, therefore, have little hesitation in placing it to the account of Scribe C.

Finally, we need, I think, feel as little hesitation in attributing the perfunctory act and scene-divisions in the F1 text to the same hand. All the printed headings we have are: *Actus Primus, Scœna Prima* (which the F1 compositors would set up automatically), *Scena Secunda, Scena Tertia* (with nothing for scenes 4 and 5), *Actus Secundus* (the *Scena Prima* being omitted), *Scena Secunda*—and the rest is silence. It would seem from this that Scribe C set out with some intention of entering up the divisions fully because he thought they were required in print. That he did not persist for long is in keeping with his carelessness elsewhere. But had he found such divisions in the prompt-book, we can hardly doubt that even so casual a copyist would have at least entered up the five acts. In any event, no divisions of any kind are to be found in Q2 and presumably they were also absent from Shakespeare's manuscript.[1]

---

[1] On the general question of act-divisions in play-books and on the stage *vide Review of English Studies*, 1926, 1927, 1928.

CHAPTER III

The Character of the Second Quarto Text

§ VI. THE COPY FOR *HAMLET*, 1605 AND ITS COMPOSITOR

Having noted the symptoms of F1 we are now in a position to diagnose its disease as one of double transcription, particularly acute in the later stages. Turning to Q2, we seem at first to be confronted with a text even more corrupt than the other. The *Hamlet* of 1623 is, superficially at least, a clean piece of work; that is to say, it is well printed. The *Hamlet* of 1605, on the other hand, so teems with misprints, with strange spellings, with missing letters, and with omitted words, lines and passages, that perusal of a single page is likely to inspire the uninitiated with distaste and distrust. Little wonder that editors before the days of critical bibliography treated it as a kind of textual ruin, itself beyond repair, though useful as a quarry for the supply of readings to the F1 version. Yet, while the condition of the F1 *Hamlet* seems to grow worse the more we look into it, that of the "good" Q2 happily improves upon acquaintance. Its disorders are manifold but nothing like so deep-seated as its rival's, and are therefore the more amenable to editorial treatment. In other words, the malady of the 1623 *Hamlet*, a malady which had gone far before it reached the printer's hands, was corrupt copy; that of the 1605 *Hamlet* belongs in the main to the printing-house, though partly also to difficulties in the copy for which Shakespeare himself must be held responsible.

(a) Shakespeare's manuscript

Our argument has hitherto proceeded on the assumption that this copy, the copy used by James Roberts for the printing of Q2 in 1605, was either a manuscript in the author's own hand, or a faithful transcript from such a manuscript; and everything we have had occasion to observe about it in comparison with the F1 text tends to bear this out. The revelation of the true character of that text itself still further encourages us to believe it; for an original *Hamlet* manuscript in Shakespeare's autograph must have existed at some time or other; what became of it? It was certainly not printed in F1, nor was it made use of in any way on the occasion of that printing. Is it not natural to suppose, therefore, that it had already served as copy for the text printed in 1605?

When Dr Pollard labelled this a "good" quarto, he had chiefly in mind the conditions of its publication, which, unlike those of its "bad" relation of 1603, were thoroughly respectable, and suggest that James Roberts procured his copy from the players themselves.[1] The printer, indeed, claims on his title-page that his text is "according to the true and perfect Coppie", and we have no reason to doubt his word. Moreover, having gone to the trouble of making out a clean prompt-book from Shakespeare's draft, as we have seen they did, the acting company could afford to send that draft to the printer. They assuredly would not hand over the prompt-book they had just made; nor, as the difference in stage-directions, etc., in the two texts testify, did they go to the further trouble of copying out that prompt-book for him. Had they known that in the days to come a manuscript in Shakespeare's hand would be priceless, the thrifty fellows might have guarded their treasure more carefully. They could not know this. On the

---

[1] *Vide Shakespeare Folios and Quartos*, pp. 73–4.

contrary, having in the prompt-book a far more legible and what no doubt seemed to them a more actable version, they would probably take no further interest in the original manuscript, and might dispatch it to the press without scruple.

Everything we know or can surmise about the theatre library of that age renders this interpretation likely enough. In 1925 Dr Greg discovered a reference to "the fowle papers of the Authors" in a transcript of Beaumont and Fletcher's *Bonduca* at the British Museum, and thus established the fact that the original manuscript of a dramatist's play might be preserved in the theatre side by side with the prompt-book which had been copied from it by the book-holder or other playhouse scribe.[1] Following this up, in an important paper on "The Elizabethan Printer and Dramatic Manuscripts", read before the Bibliographical Society and published in December 1931, Dr McKerrow advanced the theory that plays of the period were generally printed, not from prompt-copies which the players would be unlikely to let out of their hands, but from the authors' originals, and that the "fowle" state of such papers would account for the striking inferiority of printed plays to all contemporary products of the printing-house.[2] Whether this theory be applicable to Shakespearian texts in general I do not know, nor is this the occasion to enquire; but it certainly fits the facts of the *Hamlet* texts. That it was found necessary to make a clean copy for performance shows that in the case of *Hamlet* the autograph draft was not, as we have been apt to assume in regard to other plays, suitable for prompt-book service. And that this draft was to some extent "fowle" we can hardly doubt. The tangles and cruxes already considered witness it, while no small share of the imperfections of the Q2 text, which we are

---

[1] *Prompt Copies, Private Transcripts, and the Playhouse Scrivener* in *The Library*, VI, 148–56.

[2] *Ibid.* XII, 253–75.

about to examine, may be set down to the difficulty of the printer's copy.

For the internal evidence in favour of a Shakespearian manuscript being handled by the printers of 1605 is no less striking than the external. Nineteenth-century editors described the text of Q2 as more "literary" than that of F1. The epithet was ill-chosen; there is nothing distinctively literary about Q2. Shakespeare was a working dramatist, who always thought in terms of the stage, and never so far as we know ever contemplated any other kind of publication for his plays than that which stage-performance gives. Nevertheless, it is certainly true to say that Q2 is less "theatrical" than F1. Our review of the stage-directions in the two texts in § III has illustrated this. Everywhere we found the directions in Q2 vaguer and less stagey than those of F1, while on the other hand the F1 directions were often seen to be less subtle and less dramatic than their Q2 parallels. Further, Q2 is almost entirely free from any trace of the prompter's hand. There is only one piece of evidence which suggests that it may have been read with a view to performance, and that is the duplication of a stage-direction at 5.2.294. Here Q2 prints:

> *Drum, trumpets and shot.*
> *Florish, a peece goes off.*

And it seems likely that one of these directions (probably the first, since the second is anticipated in almost identical words in a direction at 1.4.6) was added in the margin by the prompter while reading through the text, in order to make sure that important "business off" was not forgotten.[1] And if we ask when he did this, the answer must surely be that he was reading the manuscript preparatory to the making out of the prompt-book. Another conceivable indication of the prompter's handling of the original manuscript is the

---

[1] This was frequently done in dramatic MSS. of the time; cf. Greg, *Elizabethan Dramatic Documents*, p. 213.

remarkable direction at the head of 4.1, referred to on p. 38, together with the unnecessary entry of Rosencrantz and Guildenstern at this point. The anomaly is perhaps best explained by some episode being omitted or cut out between the two scenes. But such adaptation may very well have been the work of Shakespeare himself in the course of revision; and if so it belongs to the history of the *Hamlet* text in the sixteenth century, which lies outside the scope of the present enquiry.[1] As for the passages which we know to have been omitted from Q2 because we have them in F1, none of them appears to have been left out for any theatrical reason. One omission, as we shall see, was certainly accidental, and the rest may well have been accidental also.

To my mind, the strongest evidence for the authenticity of the copy for Q2 is the fact that it preserves untampered with those textual tangles and cruxes which, as the F1 text shows, the prompter attempted, with varying success, to straighten out. In a word, the very roughness of the Q2 text is its best guarantee. The peculiar spellings of which, as we shall presently see, the text is full are part of the same phenomenon, as are also the numerous misprints. All may be paralleled in other "good" Shakespearian texts, and are just the kind of spelling and misprint which we are accustomed to look for in printed plays probably set up from MSS. in Shakespeare's hand. Finally, the absence of act and scene-divisions and the light punctuation are both characteristic of Shakespeare, and both are violently handled in the F1 version.

To sum up, there is a high probability that the copy delivered to James Roberts at the beginning of the seventeenth century by the Globe company was Shakespeare's own manuscript. Probability is not proof; and, while we can prove (as I hope my readers will agree) that the copy for the F1 *Hamlet* was a transcript from the prompt-book, we can postulate nothing for certain about the copy for Q2.

[1] *Vide* p. xvi.

Nevertheless, the theory that the book published early in 1605[1] was printed from Shakespeare's autograph is a sound working hypothesis, which grows the more persuasive the more we study the Q2 text. I shall not hesitate to build upon it in what follows.

(b) The compositor and his ways

Shakespeare's manuscript of *Hamlet* was, I have suggested, at once too difficult and too confused to be of any use as a prompt-book. And it is well to reiterate the supposition here, since we can afford to make every possible allowance for the workmen in Roberts' office, who in the quarto of 1605 gave us one of the worst printed of all the original Shakespearian texts.

Some of what is wrong is due to imperfect press-work and nothing else. We find, for example, letters disappearing at the end of extra-long lines. There are three certain instances of this happening, and in two of them different extant copies[2] of Q2 give us these lines in different states. Thus the last word of 1.1.91 (sig. B2 *verso*) in all copies appears as "returne" instead of "returned", while at 1.5.7 (sig. D2 *verso*) some copies give us "heare." and others "hear", and at 1.2.213 (sig. C2 *verso*) some copies "watch" and others "watcl". This third example is of special interest inasmuch as what I represent as "l" is really a half-printed "h", and the fact that F1 reads "watcht" at first suggested that a "t" had also failed to print, until I discovered a comma after a slightly blurred "h" in the Grimston copy, a discovery which established "watch," as the true reading.[3] The fact that these letters all occur at the ends of lines of extra length, and lines three or four

---

[1] For the date of publication *vide* p. 124.

[2] For particulars of these copies and the names here given for them see below, p. 122.

[3] Cf. vol. II, p. 263. There seems also to be a comma in the Capell copy.

from the top of the *verso* of the second leaf of a sheet, or in other words at the same point of three consecutive outer formes (B, C, D), and that in the B.M. copy the "bite" of the second and blind half of the "h" is clearly visible, proves that the eclipse of the letters was caused by the edge of the frisket overlapping the type a little and so preventing it leaving an inked impression on the paper.[1] But the same explanation will not account for the absence of other letters or of words such as we get in "why she" for "Why she, euen she" at the end of 1.2.149, the omission of "Then senselesse Illium" at the end of 2.2.496, and "cowards" for "Cowards of vs all" at the end of 3.1.83. Furthermore, these omissions are only a handful out of a large number which may occur at the beginning, the middle or any other part of the line. It is obvious, therefore, that for such omissions we must find another cause.

There is something very odd about the compositor's work in this book; disgraceful as it is as a piece of printing, its punctuation, as we shall see, is on the whole excellent, while it is surprisingly free from what may be called normal compositors' slips. I have observed only one example of "literal" misprinting ("thrre" for "there" at 4.3.36), seven examples of turned letters, all of the *n* : *u* type, and therefore alternatively to be explained as minim-misreadings,[2]† three of transposed letters ("retrogard" 1.2.114, "rehume" 2.2.529, "spend thirfts" 4.7.123),† and two of superfluous letters, viz. "imploratotors" at 1.3.129 and "againgst" at 5.2.155, parallels to which may be found in almost any book of the period. The shortness of this list suggests that the compositor's type-case was in good order and that he

---

[1] For "forme" *vide* below, p. 125 n., and for "bite" and "frisket" *vide* McKerrow, *Introd. to Bibliography*, pp. 16–17. I owe the explanation given above to a suggestion in a letter from Dr J. Q. Adams of the Folger Shakespeare Library, Washington, and was able to confirm it by inspection of the B.M. copy.

[2] Cf. pp. 106–7, 118, below.

ought to have been a careful workman. Turn, however, to omitted letters, and you get a very different notion of his quality. The text contains no less than thirty-two instances of this fault; and, though some of them are doubtful and a few such as "shone" for "showne" and "bettles" for "beetles" may be spellings and not misprints, there can be no disputing that in most cases letters which the compositor intended to set up in his stick are missing.[1] Why should an apparently competent compositor leave out all these letters?

To answer this question properly we must enquire a little more closely into what went on in Roberts' office at the end of 1604. And when we do so, we find that not merely are letters absent from the text but words, not merely words but phrases, not merely phrases but whole lines, and not merely lines but passages, some of considerable length. Here are the facts and the figures:[2]

> Verbal omissions = 96 instances
>   (certain = 53, probable = 43).
> Omission of lines or half-lines = 29 instances.
> Omission of passages = 83 lines.
> Total number of lines affected = 208.

It is the omitted passages, naturally enough, which have attracted the special attention of editors in the past, and various reasons have been advanced to account for them. But to consider them in isolation is to miss the clue to them, and no one has hitherto realised that they are only part of a malady which afflicts the Q2 text as a whole. In short, omission—omission of letters, of words, of phrases, of lines, and of extended passages—is one of the outstanding bibliographical facts of the book. And this being so, it is surely only common sense to look for a common cause for the whole related phenomena. This cause I find in the compositor being driven to exceed his proper speed of work in the setting up of a very difficult manuscript.

[1] *Vide* the list on p. 118.   [2] *Vide* the lists (vol. II, pp. 244–51).

Imagine a hurried compositor, and all the defects just noted are accounted for. No doubt we must distinguish. The omission of letters and words, of word-groups and of lines, may have been and probably was inadvertent. Working against time, I suggest, the eye of the man skipped words and phrases in his copy, while his fingers leaped the boxes in his case. But inadvertence will not explain his leaving out lengthy passages. And here, I think, the omission may have been deliberate and perhaps dishonest. Given the undue pressure, the temptation to shorten the task by ignoring parts of the copy must have been very strong, and when we pass the omitted passages in review it is difficult to avoid agreeing with Furnivall, who wrote as long ago as 1885, "That most, if not all of the omissions of Q2 were...due to the copier or printer, is certain in some cases, and almost certain or probable in all".[1] On the other hand, they would be accounted for if the manuscript was at these places even more illegible than usual (through crowding, insertions, or the like), or it may even be that extra slips of paper were lost.[2]

The passages of any length which are found in F1 but not in Q2 are these:

(i) 2.2.244–76 A portion of the dialogue between Hamlet, Rosencrantz and Guildenstern, in which Hamlet declares that "Denmark's a prison", and his school-fellows sound him on the subject of his ambition.

(ii) 2.2.352–79. The passage concerning those "little eyases", the Children of the Chapel at the Blackfriars, and the War of the Theatres (1599–1601) in which they were engaged.

(iii) 4.5.161–3, which runs in F1:

> Nature is fine in Loue, and where 'tis fine,
> It sends some precious instance of it selfe
> After the thing it loues.

---

[1] *Vide* p. v of Griggs' Facsimile of *Hamlet* 1605.
[2] A suggestion I owe to Mrs Murrie.

(iv) 5.1.39–42, which runs in F1:

Other. Why he had none.

Clo. What, ar't a Heathen? how dost thou vnderstand the Scripture? the Scripture sayes Adam dig'd; could hee digge without Armes?

(v) 5.2.68–80. The conclusion of the dialogue between Hamlet and Horatio immediately before the entrance of Osric; a passage which breaks off in the middle of a sentence, and can have been omitted by the compositor alone, accidentally or in order to abridge his labours.

The first thing to notice about these omissions is that they *are* omissions and not passages which may have been added later to the F1 text. The second of them must have been written when the War of the Theatres was at its height, and cannot therefore have been added after the publication of Q2 in 1605 or even after 1602 when Roberts may have first received the copy from the Globe.†
The first, the fourth and the fifth of them, again, have left frayed edges behind in the Q2 text. The absence of the first passage, for example, causes ll. 243 and 277 to stand thus in juxtaposition:

Ham. Then is Doomes day neere, but your newes is not true;
But in the beaten way of friendship, what make you at Elsonoure?—

where the repeated "but" and the sudden turn of the subject clearly point to an omission. In the case of the third alone is there no indisputable proof of omission, but where passages have been demonstrably left out in four other places, we may assume that the same thing has happened here also.

It is, moreover, probable, I think, that the Q2 compositor was alone responsible for all five omissions. Some have attributed the first two to the censorship. And we do well to remember that the copy for *Hamlet* had been entered to James Roberts in the Stationers' Register for 1602 "under the handes of master Pasfield", that is to say, of the

Bishop of London's reader of books. Nor is it difficult to imagine such a censor, if he read the book after March 1603, objecting to the first of the omitted passages, seeing that the words "Denmark's a prison" might seem derogatory to the reigning Queen, Anne of Denmark,[1] while the dialogue is so close knit at this point that deletion once begun could hardly stop short of thirty lines. It has also been supposed that the second passage which reflects unfavourably, or might have been taken as reflecting unfavourably, upon the Children of the Chapel, who on the accession of James I had become the Children of the Queen's Revels, was censored for the same reason, though as a matter of fact the War of the Theatres was such stale matter when the copy was handed over to Roberts that the players themselves may have deleted the reference. It is conceivable, then, that two out of the five excisions had been carried out before the copy came into the printer's hands at all, though I personally feel it is just as probable that they were left out by the compositor, as was certainly the case with the other three. Not that it makes any difference from the editorial standpoint which hypothesis we adopt. For one thing may be said with confidence, that not a single omission in Q2, with the possible exception of 2.2.352–79, had any connection with the Globe playhouse.

I am inclined, then, to attribute the omissions of these lengthy passages, together with most of the other omissions in the Q2 text, to undue haste on the part of the compositor. I speak of "the compositor", because the imperfections of this text are so uniformly distributed throughout that it is hardly conceivable that they belong to two different workmen. And if a reason be sought for this undue haste, it will be found, I believe, by examining the spellings and misprints for which the compositor was also responsible. These

---

[1] Cf. p. 26, where the susceptibilities of Anne are suggested as a possible cause for omission in F1. Can they have affected both texts at different places?

spellings and misprints, which are of the utmost importance
for the editing not only of *Hamlet* but of Shakespearian
texts generally, will be considered in detail below.[1] We
must, however, anticipate a little for the purpose of the
argument.

First, then, Q2 is full of strange spellings, which would
seem totally illiterate to most modern readers, but which
tally so closely, on the one hand, with spellings found in
other Shakespearian quartos and in folio plays like *Antony
and Cleopatra*, which were probably printed direct from
Shakespearian manuscripts, and on the other hand with the
spellings in those Three Pages of *Sir Thomas Moore* which
many of us believe to be in Shakespeare's handwriting, that
there can be little doubt of their being for the most part
copy-spellings, i.e. spellings belonging to Shakespeare himself. In that age, when every gentleman spelt as he liked,
the spelling of manuscripts differed from author to author
and often even from page to page with the same author.
Compositors, therefore, who wished to get through their
day's work at all, neglected the spellings of their authors
and translated them into the received spelling of their
printing-house, as they carried the words in their heads. It
follows that a skilful and swift workman would rarely,
except by accident, let his copy-spellings slip into print. The
fact, then, that so many strange spellings occur in Q2 is a
sign that the compositor was neither skilful nor swift.
Secondly, Q2 is equally full of strange misprints which,
when classified, are found to conform both to the types of
misprint occurring in other good Shakespearian texts and
to the pen-slips evident in the Three Pages aforesaid. In
a word, almost all the imperfections, apart from the
omissions, in this very imperfectly printed text may be
accounted for if we imagine a slow-moving compositor at
work upon a difficult manuscript in Shakespeare's handwriting and Shakespeare's spelling. They at once strengthen

[1] *Vide* pp. 102–17.

our faith in the authenticity of the Q2 copy and tell us something about the compositor who handled it.

A few pages back we were thinking of him as working at immoderate speed and so skipping words and letters by the bushel; now he appears as a plodder, reproducing his copy letter by letter and, when (as often) he cannot read a word, setting it up in a form which is as much like a typographical facsimile of the letters in the manuscript before him as he can make it. The two pictures are not incompatible. Rather the one explains the other. What we have to deal with in Q2 is, I suggest, a learner or a young journeyman, a compositor who *cannot* work quickly because he has not mastered his craft. He has learnt neither his printing-house spelling nor the art of carrying more than one word at a time in his head. Why he was compelled to force the pace beyond his capacity we do not know; perhaps he was on piece-rate and anxious to have his task over, or perhaps his boss, James Roberts, was overdriving him, in order to get on to the next book. Anyhow, he makes a pretty mess of the autograph copy of the most famous dramatic poem in the world. He was of course completely unconscious of its beauties and subtleties. On the contrary, he probably cursed it as a pack of foul papers written in a crabbed hand. For, as I have said, Shakespeare himself must share the responsibility.

Yet, indifferent workman as the compositor was, an editor should rather have him to deal with a dozen times over than the careless copyist who prepared the transcript for the F1 text, or even the more canny and conscientious book-holder responsible for the original Globe prompt-book. He possessed neither understanding nor interest in the play he was dealing with, except in so far as it was material for wage-earning. He was concerned merely with the letters he saw, or thought he saw, in the copy, and his sole desire was to set them up in type as quickly as he could. His not to reason why; emendation was not his affair; and if a passage did not make sense, that was the author's business. For all this we ought to be profoundly thankful. "Textual critics", writes Dr Greg, "should praise God for the simple fool."[1] The fool who set up the Q2 of *Hamlet* was simple to transparency. We have only to study his little ways, and we can see through him almost every time. Even the most ludicrous of his misprints may tell us something about the Shakespearian manuscript he was handling. We may almost steal his eyes and watch Shakespeare's pen moving across the paper.

And after all, except perhaps in respect of his long omissions, he seems to have tried to do his best; that is to say, he attempted to reproduce with fidelity that which he saw before him. What proves this, and what will, I think, be regarded as his most signal service to our knowledge of Shakespeare, is his punctuation. I say "his" punctuation, but it was not his, or at least only his to a small degree. For it is clear that, just as he could not spell and had never learnt the head-carrying process, so also he had no punctuation of his own, beyond some acquaintance with the use of the comma. Thus he was obliged to rely almost entirely upon the punctuation of his copy, which, apart from some obvious deviations and not a few omissions, he followed as closely as he did the forms of the letters. In other words, we have in the Q2 *Hamlet* not only a rich mine of information about Shakespeare's penmanship and spelling, but also what I believe to be (almost untampered with) a whole play—and what a play!—punctuated throughout as Shakespeare had punctuated it in his manuscript.[2]

If only the plodding, literal compositor had been left alone to do his best and his worst! The tragedy of *Hamlet*, 1605, from the editor's point of view is that he was not. His master, Roberts, or some other superior person in the

[1] *The Library*, Sept. 1932, p. 125.
[2] *Vide* vol. II, pp. 192–215 for a detailed discussion of punctuation in Q2 and F1.

printing-house, unfortunately discovered, from inspection both of his proofs and of his sheets while they were being struck off the press, how disastrously things were going, and tried to some extent to clean up the mess. We have, in short, to reckon not only with the untutored compositor but also with his press-corrector; and it is the corrector who gives an editor most of his trouble. For he is not a want-wit like his junior; he knows, for instance, or fancies he knows, what a line of verse means; and he is anxious to make sense out of such nonsense as catches his eye. On the other hand, he never seems to think of consulting the original copy when in doubt, and he emends according to the light of his own intelligence; so that, though fortunately to a far smaller degree, his influence is as baneful after the same fashion as that of the two scribes in the F1 text. His sophistication of the simple folly of the compositor is so important textually that it demands a separate section to itself. Let us first, however, explore further the work of the transparent journeyman as evidenced by classified lists of the spellings and misreadings in Q2, which must be considered in their turn as part of the whole body of misprints in that text.

(c) Misprints and spellings in the good quarto

Working, as his inexperience compelled him, from letter to letter rather than from word to word, and compelled too, in his haste, generally to begin a fresh word before he had grasped the meaning of that which he had just finished, the compositor probably seldom if ever appreciated the sense of the lines he was setting up in his stick. On five occasions, at least, as we have already seen,[1] his memory tricked him into repeating a word he had set up the moment before. At others, when perhaps the copy looked deceptively easy, or

[1] *Vide* p. 51.

after an interval for refreshment from "a stoup of ale", his eagerness to get on with the job might cause him to guess at the whole word from a glimpse of its first syllable, or his eye might conceivably race ahead of his fingers, so that he caught a word from the end of a line and set it up unconsciously near the beginning.[1]

Impatience of this kind is probably the best explanation of transpositions like the following:

3.2.409

(Q2) And doe such busines as the bitter day
(F1) And do such bitter businesse as the day

3.4.89

(Q2) Thou turnst my very eyes into my soule
(F1) Thou turn'st mine eyes into my very soule

4.7.126

(Q2) To showe your selfe indeede your fathers sonne
(F1) To show your selfe your Fathers sonne indeede—

or of this interesting misprint, to which we shall return later[2] and in which, I think, we can see the compositor guessing at a word from a hurried glance:

3.1.160

(Q2) Th'expectation, and Rose of the faire state
(F1) Th'expectansie and Rose of the faire State.

There was indeed much in the copy to lead the luckless compositor astray. It was, for instance, full of strange words and strange forms, such as "expectansie", which he had probably never seen before.

But it was seemingly Shakespeare's penmanship and archaic orthography which gave him most trouble, with results highly interesting to anyone with an assiduous curiosity concerning the way in which Shakespeare formed his letters and spelt his words. Indeed, the misreadings and

---

[1] *Vide* pp. 54–5.   [2] *Vide* pp. 163–4.

peculiar spellings of Q2 belong to the same textual malady, and cannot rightly be considered the one apart from the other. To take a simple illustration, the compositor seems to halt between the terminations -*ction* and -*xion*, while in "complextion" (1.4.27) we have what looks like a hybrid of the two forms. Hybrid and hesitation, however, are both explained if we suppose that Shakespeare himself vacillated between -*xion*, for which the appearance of "fixion" in both Q2 and F1 (2.2.578) is fair evidence, and the old-fashioned termination -*ccion*, for which we have evidence both in *Love's Labour's Lost*[1] and in the "Shakespearian" Addition to *Sir Thomas More*.[2] At the opposite extreme we may take an example in which a strange word, a strange spelling and careless handwriting seem to have combined to baffle the compositor completely. At 5.1.97 Shakespeare evidently wrote "masserd" for "mazzard", but forming, as he often did, his *r* like an *n* and his *d* like an *e*; so that the compositor, entirely at sea, set it up as "massene". Among other nonsense words or expressions of the same kind may be mentioned: somnet (sp. sommet = summit, 1.4.70 and 3.3.18), the vmber (thumbes, 3.2.373), kyth (tythe, 3.4.97), bord (bore, 4.6.26), loued Arm'd (loud a wind, 4.7.22), the King (checking, 4.7.63), trennowed (sp. wennowed = winnowed, 5.2.200); and in each case it will be noticed how closely the misprint conforms to the spelling and shape of the original word. Not that the compositor always makes nonsense. At times, "as the blind man catcheth a hare", he hits a plausible reading, which is all the more dangerous for so being. A good instance among a number is the variant at 5.2.17–18, where F1 reads "vnseale Their grand Commission" and Q2 "vnfold Their graund commission". Most editors follow F1 to avoid the rhyme with "bold" in the previous line; but Jennens, Elze and Halliwell read "unfold" with Q2; and the matter might

---

[1] *Vide* p. 103 *L.L.L.* ("New Shakespeare").
[2] *Vide Shakespeare's Hand in the Play of "Sir Thomas More"*, p. 127.

have remained for ever in doubt had we not come to
recognise how easy it would be for this compositor to misread "sele" as "fold" in Shakespeare's handwriting.

Similarly the transformation of "revel" into "reueale"
(1.4.17) would be natural enough at the beginning of the
seventeenth century; for if Shakespeare wrote "revele", as
well he might, he presented the compositor with an am-
biguous form. Had the latter paused to consider the context
he would have seen at once that

This heauy headed reueale east and west

was beside the mark; but he was in haste, took his shot, and
passed on. In like fashion the spelling "leve" (live), a not
uncommon one in the sixteenth century, helps us to understand how the compositor came to set up "live" as "leaue"
at 3.4.158, while the misprint "greeued" for "grained" at
l. 90 of the same scene amounts almost to proof that
"greined" was the form that Shakespeare wrote, a spelling
very easily mistaken for "greiued" and so printed "greeued".
And there are many other instances of the kind, which will
best be considered in connection with the general body of
misreadings in Q2. Before, however, discussing misreadings in detail, a cautionary word must be said upon the
phenomenon in general. The lists that follow, as indeed the
qualifications here and there expressed should make clear,
are not intended to be accepted in any absolute sense. I am
convinced that misreading of Shakespeare's handwriting, or
as it is sometimes called "graphic error", is one of the
major causes of corruption in the Q2 text and I believe the
lists themselves will prove this. But where there exist other
possibilities such as "turned letters", the omission of letters
or the misguided rectification of misprints on the part of
the press-corrector, it is obvious that individual misprints
are often open to alternative explanations.[1] All therefore
that inclusion in the following lists implies is that the mis-

[1] Cf. below, pp. 118, 147.

print in question probably or possibly arose through mis-reading by the compositor of a word in Shakespeare's manuscript, taking as a sample of such manuscript the Three Pages in the *Booke of Sir Thomas Moore* now accepted by many as Shakespearian.

A. *Misreadings*[1]

The commonest misprints in the printed Shakespearian texts, together with the commonest pen-slips in the Three Pages of *Sir Thomas Moore*, fall into five classes. Taking them in turn, we may note the parallels in *Hamlet* as we go along:

(i) *minim* errors. In the "English" script that Shake-speare wrote, minim-letters, i.e. letters formed of more or less straight strokes, are *m, n, u, i, c, r, w*; and the large number of compositor's errors in words containing such letters prove that he must have been more than ordinarily careless in the formation of them, that he did not properly distinguish between the convex and concave forms, and that he often kept no count of his strokes, especially when writing two or more minim-letters in combination. For example, we have "game" for "gain" (*Oth.* 5.1.14), "comming" for "cunning" (*T.C.* 3.2.140), "vncharmd" for "unharmed" and "fennell" for "female" (*Rom.* 1.1 217, 1.2.29), "smiles" for "similes" and "trustfull for "tristful" (1 *Hen. IV*, 1.2.89, 2.4.434), "blacks" for "blanks" (*Son.* 77.10).

Hamlet. (a) *n:u*—2.2.1, etc. Rosencraus (Rosencrantz), 1.2.83 deuote (denote), 1.3.76 loue (loan), 1.5.77 vnanueld

---

[1] This list, which includes only obvious misprints corrected in all modern editions, has been to some extent anticipated in the present writer's Textual Introduction to *The Tempest* ("New Shakespeare"), in his article *Spellings and Misprints in the Second Quarto of Hamlet*, in *Essays and Studies of the English Association*, vol. x (pp. 41–46), and in *Shakespeare's Hand in "Sir Thomas More"*, pp. 117–120.

(unaneled), 2.2.450 Fankners (falconers), 3.1.119 euocutat (inoculate), 3.4.90 greeued (grained), 4.7.78 ribaud (riband). All but the first of these have been referred to above under the head of Turned Letters (*vide* p. 94), a phenomenon which obviously offers an alternative explanation. (b) *m, n, u, i*— 1.2.137 thus (this), 5.1.308 this (thus). These again may be compositor's slips rather than misreadings. 5.2.226 gamgiuing (gain-giving), 1.4.70, 3.3.18 somnet (summit), 3.1.166 time (tune), 3.2.147 munching (miching), 3.4.20 the most (th'inmost), 3.4.160 assune (assume). (c) *c : minim* —2.2.214 sanctity (sanity), 2.2.339 black (blank), 3.2.2 pronoun'd (pronounc'd), 4.7.14 concliue (conjunctive). Here once more the alternative possibility of omitted letters must be borne in mind. (d) *r : minim*—3.2.179 Lord (love), 5.1.109 madde (rude), 4.7.135 ore (on), 3.4.88 pardons (pandars), 5.1.97 massene (mazzard), 2.2.280 euer (even), 2.2.585 her (Hecuba), 1.1.121 feare (fierce), 2.2.469 when (where), 2.1.38 wit (warrant), 3.4.6 wait (warrant). (e) *w : minim*—4.7.22 arm'd (a wind), 5.1.94 went (meant), 3.1.196 vnmatcht (unwatched), 3.1.46 lowlines (loneliness), 3.3.58 showe (shove).

From this group of misprints we may, I think, infer the following Shakespearian spellings: Rosencrans, lone, faukners, sommet, greined, enoculat, one (on), masserd, fearce, wher (where), ment. Other errors may be readily explained if we bear in mind abbreviated or syncopated forms. Thus the hypothetical "thinmost" (th'inmost), with a minim or two short, will account for "the most";[1] a contracted "hec" for "Hecuba"[2] gives us a possible origin of the curious "her"; the occurrence at 1.2.243 of the syncopated "warn't" for "warrant" shows us how the word

---

[1] Cf. the F1 misprint "their corporall" (th'incorporall) at 3.4.118.

[2] It should perhaps be noted that this name occurs three times in two consecutive lines, and it was when Shakespeare had to write it for the third time that he contracted it. *Vide* Greg, *Emendation*, p. 57 (*Aspects*, p. 184) for a different explanation.

came to be misprinted first "wit" and then "wait";[1] and we can even juggle "conjunctive" out of "concliue" by supposing that Shakespeare wrote some kind of contracted form in the manuscript. The strangest looking transformations are often simple enough once the minim business is understood; figure out, for example, the misprint "arm'd" < "a wind", minim-stroke for minim-stroke, and nothing could be more straightforward.

Finally, we have a small group of instances comprising double or even treble misprints, so that they will reappear in the classes that follow. Thus "lord" < "loue" and "massene" < "masserd" are *e:d* as well as *r:minim* errors; "pardons" < "pandars" not only illustrates, both ways on, the *n:r* confusion, but the *a:o* confusion likewise; and in "madde" < "rude" we have an example of the *a:u* class, which we must now examine.

(ii) *a:minim* errors. This second class is closely connected with the first, and is to be explained by Shakespeare's frequent habit (well illustrated in the Three Pages) of curving the initial minim of *u* so that the letter looked like an ill-formed *a*, or conversely, and less frequently, of leaving the top of his *a* open. Thus *Oth.* (4.1.72, 1.3.166) gives us "coach" for "couch" and "heate" for "hint" (sp. "hente"); *T.C.* (1.3.252, 2.3.275) "seat" for "sense" and "call" for "cull"; and *L.L.L.* (4.2.95, 5.2.352) "pecas" for "pecus" and "vnsallied" for "unsullied".

Hamlet—2.2.54, etc. Gertrard (Gertrude), 1.2.105 course (corse), 2.1.39 sallies (sullies), 2.2.628 (2) deale (devil), 3.1.75 quietas (quietus), 3.3.22 raine (ruin), 3.4.59 heaue, a (heaven), 5.1.109 madde (rude), 5.1.239 waters (winter's).

---

[1] Dr Greg suggests that "warrant" may have been contracted as "wrᵗ" (2.1.38) and as "warᵗ" (3.4.6), which would give us "wit" and "wait" simply enough. The word appears as "write" in *All's Well* (F1) 3.5.69, "warne" in *A.Y.L.* (F1) 4.1.77 and "warnd" in *M.N.D.* (Q1) 5.1.326.

It is clear from this interesting group that the Q2 compositor was liable to confuse Shakespeare's *a*'s and *u*'s, and "raine" < "ruin", "heaue, a" < "heaven" are beautiful specimens. This point is important, in so far as quite a number of the serious cruxes in the text really fall, as I shall hope to show, within the *a : minim* class. For the rest, "course" and "deale" establish the Shakespearian spellings "coarse" and "deule", the second of which as a matter of fact occurs elsewhere in Q2, i.e. at 3.2.137, while the former is found in F1 at 1.2.105 and 1.4.52.

(iii) *e : d* errors. As has already been noted, the formation of these two letters generally differs as regards scale only, in the English style, a difference which the quantity of misprints due to confusion between them in the quartos and F1 proves that Shakespeare was not careful to observe. A few oddities may here be quoted: "end" for "due" (*Son.* 69.3); "beholds" for "behowls" (*M.N.D.* 5.1.379), where the spelling "behoules" was no doubt misread "beholds"; "some" for "fond" (*Rom.* 4.5.82); "and" for "are" and "one" for "are" (2 *Hen. IV*, 1.3.71, 1.2.196). Similar carelessness is to be found in almost every line of the Three Pages.

Hamlet—1.1.94 desseigne (design'd), 3.2.33 praysd (praise), 3.3.50 pardon (pardon'd), 3.3.75 reuendge (reveng'd), 4.5.38 ground (grave), 4.6.26 bord (bore), 4.7.6 proceede (proceeded), 4.7.22 loued (loud), 5.2.52 Subscribe (Subscrib'd), 3.2.179 Lord (love), 5.1.97 massene (mazzard).

None of these needs particular remark, though it should be noted that "pardon", "proceede" and possibly "desseigne", "reuendge"† and "subscribe" may be due to omission. The word "loude" has, I suggest, been read as "loued".

(iv) *e : o* errors. The small-scale *e* and *o* are very similar in English script; they are therefore liable to confusion in rapid writing. Thus we find confusions between "these" and "those" (*T.C.* 3.2.12), "ouer" and "euer" (*2 Hen. IV*, 3.2.339), "then" and "thou" (*Rom.* 3.3.52), "left" and "lost" (*Oth.* 4.2.46, 47), "now" and "new" (*Ado*, 3.2.61; *M.N.D.* 1.1.10), and so on.

Hamlet—1.1.88 these (those),[1] 1.2.1 (S.D.) Counsaile:as (councillors), 1.2.174, etc. Elsonoure (Elsinore), 2.2.232 euer (over), 5.1.9 so offended (se offendendo), 5.2.17 vnfold (unseal).

Here "Elsonoure" and "vnfold" reveal the copy-spellings "Elsenoure" and "vnsele", "vnfold" being a triple misprint. The guess-misprint "expectation" for "expectansie" noted above (p. 103) helps by analogy to explain "so offended". But the most interesting of the group is perhaps "Counsaile:as", which I take to be the Shakespearian "Counsailors" transmuted by a combined *e:o* and *a:minim* misprint into two words and a colon.

(v) *o:a* errors. This curious type of misprint is very neatly explained by the handwriting of the Three Pages, where we find frequent instances of the closed *a* in which the upright has become detached from the body of the letter, so as to give something closely resembling *o* linked with the letter following, or at times *oi* or even *or*. Misprints such as "doues" for "daws" (sp. "daues") in *Oth.* 1.1.65, "obiect" for "abject" and "Calcho's" for "Calchas" in *T.C.* 3.3.128, 4.1.37, "obsque" for "absque" in *2 Hen. IV*, 5.5.30, and "lost" for "last" in *Merch.* 2.2.105 illustrate the confusion; but none of the quartos has such clear evidence of the *or:a* error as *Hamlet* Q2.

Hamlet—1.2.58 *Polo.* Hath (*Pol.* He hath), 1.2.96 or minde (a mind), 1.5.56 sort (sate), 2.2.517 follies (fallies).

The "follies" misprint is included here, rather than in the *o:e* class, because F1 gives us "fallies" as the spelling of the word, though all editors print "fellies". The corruption "*Polo.* Hath" is interesting. What happened, I conjecture, was that Shakespeare wrote "Pol a hath", using

[1] This may of course be a grammatical slip, cf. vol. II, pp. 241–2.

the colloquial form of "he" as he frequently did, and that this "a" was read as part of the speech-prefix by the compositor. The fact that all Polonius' other speeches in the text are headed "*Pol.*" bears out the supposition. In "or minde", and "sort" we have clear examples of the *or : a* confusion, which will help us later with some of the cruxes of the text.

Other misreadings in Q2, which do not fall under these five main heads, may be lumped together in one group. It will be noticed that Shakespeare's *t* was a frequent source of trouble, and a reference to Maunde Thompson's plates illustrating the forms of Shakespeare's individual letters (available to students in *Shakespeare's Hand in "Sir Thomas More"*) will show how it came to be so, and how the other letters in the list might be mistaken one for another.

(vi) *Miscellaneous.*

t : e errors—*Oth.* 1.3.51 lacke (lackt), *Son.* 47.10 are (art), *Rom.* 4.1.7 talke (talkt), *Oth.* 3.3.266 valt (vale), *M.N.D.* 2.2.39 bet (bee).

Hamlet—2.2.126 about (above), 3.1.164 musickt (musicke), 3.1.167 stature (feature), 3.2.321 stare (start).

t : c errors—*Oth.* 2.3.311 ingredience (ingredient),† *T.C.* 1.1.37 scorne (storm), *L.L.L.* 5.1.52 puericia (pueritia), 5.2.817 instance (instant), *Rom.* 5.3.107 pallat (palace), *L.L.L.* 4.2.31 indistreel (indiscreet), 5.1.127 assistants (assistance).

Hamlet—4.7.63 the King (checking).

l or *t : k* errors—*T.C.* 2.3.203 liked (titled), *Merch.* 4.1.74 bleake (bleate), *Ham.* (F1) 2.2.479 to take (totall).

Hamlet—3.4.97 kyth (tythe), 4.7.20 Worke (Would). Cf. also p. 145–6 for 2.2.468 talke (tale).

t : s (final) errors—*L.L.L.* 4.2.82 sapis (sapit).

Hamlet—1.5.68 possesse (posset).

ſ : s (long) errors—This error is common in all books of the period.

Hamlet—3.1.167 stature (feature), 3.2.267 Considerat (Confederate), 5.2.17 vnfold (unseal).

l:t errors—*Rom.* 4.1.72 stay (slay), *2 Hen. IV*, 2.2.91 rabble (rabbit, sp. "rabbet"), *T.C.* 2.2.14 surely (surety).

Hamlet—2.2.228 extent (excellent), 5.2.101 sully (sultry).

l:d or *e* errors—*Rom.* 3.1.171 aged (agile), *2 Hen. IV*, 4.4.32 meeting (melting).

Hamlet—1.2.257 fonde (foul), 1.3.131 beguide (beguile).

th or *h:y* or *z* errors—*2 Hen. IV*, 2.2.18 with (viz), *Oth.* 3.3.440 it (that; taken for "yt"), *Merch.* 3.5.82 it (then; taken for "yt").

Hamlet—5.2.199 histy (yesty), 2.2.450 friendly (French), 1.1.73 with (why).

†*h:th* errors—*L.L.L.* 5.2.569 his (this), *Merch.* 4.1.30 this (his), *Lear*, 1.2.88 this (his).

Hamlet—4.5.89, 5.2.148 this (his).

e:y errors—*Rom.* 4.1.92 the (thy), *L.L.L.* 3.1.59 the (thy), *T.C.* 1.3.61 the (thy), *Oth.* 3.3.447 thy (the).

Hamlet—3.2.141 ber Lady (by'r lady), 4.7.89 me (my), 5.2.5 my (me), 4.7.168 horry (hoar, sp. "hoare").

r:s (final) errors—*L.L.L.* 3.1.182 Junios (junior).

Hamlet—3.2.373 the vmber (thumbes), 5.2.43 as sir (as'es, sp. "assis").

h:s (? long italic) errors—

Hamlet—4.6.31 So (He).

The copy-spellings "posset" (misread "posses"), "yisty", and "horre" may be inferred from three of these misprints, while in the curious "friendly" < "French" the compositor was perhaps led astray by a malformed *h*, which looked like a *y* and so presented him with a combination of letters which his eye took to be "frenly". The misprint may, however, be partly due to the press-corrector. The *e:y* confusion, not uncommon in the quartos, is apparently due to the use of the ε form, which, though unusual finally, occurs

once at least in the "Shakespearian" Three Pages
(l. 62 "peace"). Misprints like "kyth"<"tythe",
"beguide"<"beguile", "histy"<"yesty", and plenty
more of a like kind from the earlier groups show how little
the time-honoured critical canon which bids us always
prefer the more difficult of two alternative readings is to
be relied upon when we are dealing with a stupid compositor. Indeed, the moral of our collection of misreadings,
which runs to close upon ninety examples, is twofold.
It is: study (i) the habits of your compositor, and (ii) the
spellings of your author.

An examination of the misprints has already taught us
something about Shakespeare's orthography; we shall learn
more by turning to a list of all the remarkable spellings
which appear in Q2, many of which we can feel pretty
certain were conveyed by the eye and hand of the inexperienced compositor direct from the copy to his stick.[1]
This does not mean, of course, that they are all Shakespeare's. For example, there is a tendency for "will" and
"till" to be spelt "well" and "tell", "accident" and
"different" to be spelt "accedent" and "defferent", while
we get "inuected" for "infected" (3.2.269), "griefes" for
"grieves" (3.2.209) and "twelfe" for "twelue" (1.1.7,
1 2.252, 1.4.3), spellings I have not observed elsewhere in
Shakespearian texts and which may therefore belong to the
compositor himself, who in the office of a James Roberts
was conceivably a Welshman. Furthermore he certainly
normalised to some extent as he worked. We have seen him
doing so in forms like "complextion" and "complection".
Again, except for five instances of "off" (of), the text
contains no words ending in abnormal double consonants,
although spellings such as "madd", "begg", "fann",
"dirtt" occur in other Shakespearian texts and certainly

---

[1] Cf. *Shakespeare's Hand*, pp. 114–15, 122–41, and W. W. Greg,
An Elizabethan Printer and his Copy (*The Library*, IV, 102–18, Sept.
1923).

occurred in Shakespeare's manuscripts. The compositor was therefore, we may be sure, doing his best to produce a book in printing-house spelling; but he had not yet learnt to carry words in his head, his eye kept catching the letters in the copy before him, and in consequence he succeeded in preserving for us quite a considerable body of evidence on the subject of Shakespearian orthography.

B. *Spellings*

absence of final e mute: safty; wholsome; com, coms, somthing; forgon, non; thar (they're), farwell, forhead, thers (there's); els, promiscram'd; associat, confiderat (confederate), desperat, desprat, hast, hippocrit, importunat, infinit, mandat, minuts, opposits, pyrat, prenominat, smot, statuts, temperatly; trupenny; ax.

medial consonants: (a) *double*: coupple, hiddious, maddam, merrit, Parris, perrilous, plannet, pollitician, punnisht, Rennish, smilling, tennant, tirranus. (b) *single*: adicted, colection, comerse, iminent, imediate, iugled, litlest, ods, oprest, pudling, peny, puft, setled, swadling.

final -s for -sse: mistris; reckles, choples (chapless); busines, happines, highnes, lightnes, likenes, madnes, prettines, sadnes, savagenes, sicknes, tediousnes, wantonnes, weakenes, witnes, wildnes; grasgreene, grosly.

b after m: lymmes, solembe.

ck for k after n: bancke, blanck, blancket, franckly, linckt, mountibanck, pranck, ranck, sprinckle, wrinckled (cf. ancle, carbunkles, barck).

c, t, and s interchangeable before -ion, -ient, -ial: apparision, innouasion, parcial, auspitious, gratious.

c, s, and z interchangeable: blase, sellerige, choise (choice), comerse, cressant, dasie, deuise, faste (faced), incenced, orizons, pancies, pace (pass), president (precedent), pronounst, sencibly, centinels, chapes (shapes), ciz'd, cised (sized), squeesing, tradust.

-ction and *-xion*: *complection, *complextion,[1] dixion, fixion.

d before g: dirdge, harbindger, hindges, leedge, pidgion, reuendge, romadge, siedge, sindging, springde.

d and th: fadoms, tider (tether); hundreth (hundred).

g and i (*j*): iem, ierman, gelly.

s and sc: sent (scent), Sceneca (Seneca).

vowels levelled in unaccented syllables: colatural; liquer, pestur, satire (satyr), miter (metre), fingard (fingered), hazerd, perticuler, peculier, suruiuer, scholler, cullour, familier; humorus, meruiles (marvellous), sulphrus, tirranus; incestious, impitious (impetuous); angle (angel), counsaile (counsel, council), fennill, fertill, maruaile, metteld, modill, puzzels, scandle, scandell, sterill, trauaile, trauiler, vnkennill, wassel; skyesh; sommet; barraine, beckins, brazon, forraine, Lenton, recken, sexten, suddaine, sodaine; occurrants; horrable; spleenatiue; rapsedy; emphesis; windlesses; duckets; morteist; paddack; loggits; cosund; battalians; arithmaticke.

a and ai: clame, proclames, vnreclamed.

a for e: a leauen (eleven), element, marmaide, randeuous.

au for a before l: gauled, hault.

au for al: faukners, stauke.

-ay, -ey, and -ai, -ei(gh): conuay, obay, pray (prey), waigh, wey, way (weigh); cf. nabored.

e for a: dreg'd, meruiles (marvellous), sendall.

e for ai: quently.

i for ai: dintier [prob. omitted letter].

e, ee, ei, ie, ea interchangeable: compleat, cheare, deceaued, heare (here), leaprous, leasure, least (lest), preceading, reake (reck), receaue, *reueale (revel), seaz'd, seauen, shepheard, stearne, teamed, tearme, theame; beere (bier), cleere, heere (hear), neere, yeere; brest, frending,

---

[1] Spellings marked with an asterisk are either misprints or normalised forms and have already been dealt with.

ielously, nerer, peuish, tere, trecherous, wezell; cf. desseigne.

e and i: bedred, accedent, hether, indeuidible, indefferent, tell (till), well (will); confiderat (confederate), penitrable.

ee for i: spleet, week (wick), cleefe (cliff).

e and ee: step (steep), beweept, enginer, pioner.

i for ie: liue (lief).

ei for i: desseigne (design).

-ire and -ier: empier, fier, frontire.

in- and *en-*: imploy, incountred, ingaged, inough, intreate; enoculat (misp. "euocutat"), entent.

o for a: totters (tatters), rouell (ravel).

o for oa: abord, bord (*also* boord), croking, grone, lome, lothsome, rore, soke (cf. abraod, braod[1]).

o for oo: hodman, god (good), to (too).

o for u: vnwrong.

oo for o: doos, dooes, doost, doo't, fordoos, foorth, moodes (modes), prooud (proved), strooke, strooken, vphoorded, too (to).

ow for o(a): blowt, how (ho!); cf. shone (shown).

ou for u: boudge, hough (huge), ougly.

ur for ir: durt, durtie, sturre.

u and w: boule, crauling, fauning, hauke, impaunde; lowd, newtral, perswade, rowse.

u for ui and eau: butie, brute (bruit), sute.

ew for ue, ieu, or u: adew, adiew, blew, hiew, indewed, reuenew.

superfluous e mute: goblines, perhapes, snufe, youe.

miscellaneous: a (ah), arture (artery), bodkin (bodykins), conuacation (convocation), *course (corse), cride (cried), deule, *deale (devil), dosie (dizzy), heraldy (heraldry), Ierman (german), moth (mote), Pirhus (Pyrrhus), reverent (reverend), right (rite), shone (shown), shroudly (shrewdly), spight (spite), stockins (stockings), studient (student), strikt

---

[1] *Vide* p. 135.

(strict), sounds (swoons), soopstake (swopstake), twelfe (twelve), viage (voyage), yeman (yeoman).

syncopated forms: Barbry, desprat, exlent† (misprinted "extent"), medcin, nunry, poysner, poysning, sulphrus, vttrance, warn't (warrant).

abbreviations and colloquialisms: a (he), a (have), close (clothes), doo't, enso, ento't, hate (ha't), oremastret (o'ermaster it), outadoores, thar (they're), thers (there's), tho'wt, toth (to th'), toot (to't), whose (who's), woldst, woo't.

The spellings in this list, a large number of which I believe to be Shakespeare's own, strange as many of them may seem to modern eyes unaccustomed to sixteenth-century manuscripts, speak for themselves and need little comment. Taken in conjunction with the compositor's misreadings they form the groundwork of any proper study of the *Hamlet* text, and of other Shakespearian texts less rich in such evidence. In cases of corruption or of doubtful reading they are of peculiar value, since as we shall see later they enable the student to place himself more or less in the position of the original compositor by writing out the disputed word or passage in what is approximately Shakespeare's handwriting and Shakespeare's spelling, and thus in many instances to make a pretty shrewd guess as to the seat of the trouble.

By way of completing the survey of Q2 as a product of the printing-press, I now proceed to classify the other misprints of that text. In cases where alternative explanations are possible, or where two processes of corruption appear to have been at work, misprints are quoted under more than one heading.

C. *Omissions*

(i) *Of letters.* The conjectured missing letter is given in brackets. Doubtful cases are marked with a query.[1]

1.1.115 tenna[n]tlesse, 121 fear[c]e, 1.2.133 w[e]ary, 195 ?maru[a]ile, 242 to nigh[t], 1.3.48 ste[e]p (*some copies*), 1.4.71 ?be[e]ttles, 87 imag[inat]ion, 1.5.3 ?sulphr[o]us, 2.1.3 ?meru[a]iles, 2.2.76 ?sho[w]ne, 148 wat[c]h, 339 bla[n]ck, 445 by[r] lady, 582 an[d], 3.1.1 an[d], 72 ?desp[r]iz'd, 80 ?trau[a]iler, 85 ?sickl[i]ed, 3.2.2 ?pronoun[c]'d, 10 per[i]wig, 3.3.50 ?pardon[d], 4.2.6 ?Compound[ed], 4.5.106 The[y], 4.6.8 and['t], 4.7.6 ?proceede[d], 5.1.13 ?or[g]all, 68 s[t]oope, 78 d[a]intier, 205 bor[n]e, 5.2.102 [f]or, 159 re[s]ponsiue (*some copies*).

(ii) *Of words and passages.* The omitted words will be found in the lists on pp. 244–52 of vol. II, where many of them are discussed in detail. It is therefore unnecessary to print them here. It may be noted that most of them are small words, e.g. "a" is omitted five times. The omission of long passages has already been dealt with on pp. 96–8.

D. *Normal compositors' slips*

(i) *Turned letters.* It is difficult to distinguish these from *n:u* misreadings, and they have already been quoted in the first section of minim-errors above (pp. 106–7).

(ii) *Literals, etc.* (cf. p. 94).

1.2.114 retrogard, 1.3.129 imploratotors, 2.2.529 rehume, 4.3.36 thrre, 4.7.123 thirfts, 5.2.155 againgst.

(iii) *Misdivided words.* Those which are also found in F1 are so marked. Shakespeare himself may of course have been responsible for some of these.

1.2.209, F1, Whereas (Where as), 1.5.79 Withall (With all), 184 Withall (With all), 2.1.58 or tooke (oretooke), 3.4.20 the most (th'inmost), 4.7.22 arm'd (a wind),

[1] For 1.1.91 returne[d] *vide* p. 93.

63 the King (checking), 126, F1, indeede (in deed), 5.2.94 withall (with all).

(iv) *Inversions* (cf. p. 76).

3.2.409 busines as the bitter day (bitter business as the day), 3.4.89 my very eyes into my soule (my eyes into my very soul), 4.7.126 indeede your fathers sonne (your father's son in deed).

(v) *Words added.* For cases at 1.2.67, 2.2.566, and 3.2.233, cf. p. 143.

1.2.67 (much), 2.2.220 (not), 3.2.178 (Eyther none),[1] 3.2.388 (not), 3.4.215 (most).

(vi) *Repeated words* (*vide* p. 51).

1.1.45 Speake to, 2.2.390 let me, 3.4.215 most.

(vii) *Grammatical errors.*

(*a*) Confusion between sing. and plur. (verbs and subs.). Cf. vol. II, pp. 235–6. The list, which includes 23 items, is given on p. 236.

(*b*) Confusion in tense, mood, etc. See vol. II, pp. 239–40 for the list (10 items).

(*c*) Confusion in the use of pronouns. Cf. vol. II, pp. 241–2 (9 items).

3.1.165 what (that), 3.2.3 our (your), 3.2.174 our (your), 2.2.143 her (his), 4.7.106 you (him), 5.2.327 my (your), 4.7.89 me thought (my thought), 5.2.5 my thought (methought), 4.7.37 these (this).[2] Two of the last three have already been catalogued as possible misreadings.

---

[1] Cf. p. 27.
[2] *Vide* Vol. II, p. 242.

E.   *Misprints not yet accounted for* (77)

The page numbers refer to what follows.

1.1.

44 horrowes (harrows) 161–2
73 cost (cast) 149, 153, 161
107 Romeage/Romadge
      (romage) 131–2

1.2.

77 coold (good) 136
132 seale (self) 135
137 thus (to this) 142
175 for to drinke (to drink
      deep) 139

1.3.

3   in (is) 144
21 safty (sanity) 316
48 step/steepe (steep) 123
70 by/buy (buy) 123
75 boy (be) 137
77 dulleth (dulls the) 139
83 inuests (invites) 137

1.4.

49 interr'd (inurned) 149,
      154, 162
69 my/my Lord 123

1.5.

20 fearefull (fretful) 149
55 but (lust) 138
95 swiftly (stiffly) 149
116 and (bird) 138–9

2.1.

47 addission (addition) 135–6

2.2.

43 I assure (assure you) 139,
      162–3
233 lap (cap) 148
381 mouths (mows) 149
468 talke (tale) 145–6
566–7 dosen lines, or (dozen
      or) 143
587 that (the cue) 142
617 braines/braues (brains)
      123, 133

3.1.

33 Wee'le (Will) 136
107–8 you (your honesty)
      142–3
151 list (lisp) 148

3.2.

61 [*Ham.* prefix omitted] 128
94 detected (detecting) 164 n.
166 orb'd the (orbed) 141
200 the fruite (like fruit) 139
233 I be a widdow (a widow)
      143
      a wife (wife) 143
400 [*Ham.* prefix omitted] 128
407 breakes (breathes) 138

3.3.

73 but (pat) 144–5
79 silly (salary) 325

3.4.

165 to refraine night (refrain
      to-night) 143

4.3.

70 will nere begin (were ne'er begun) 144

4.5.

9 yawne (aim) 145
160 poore (old) 140

4.7.

7 criminall(crimeful)163–4
172 cull-cold (cold) 144
192 drownes (douts) 51, 137

5.1.

13 or all (argall) 138
81 into (intill) 148
213 table (chamber) 51
252 been lodg'd (have lodged) 140
260 a Requiem (sage requiem) 140
270 double (treble) 140
286 wisedom (wiseness) 149, 153, 162, 163–4
321 thirtie/thereby (shortly) 123, 125, 129

5.2.

9 pall/fall (pall) 123, 129
43 as sir (as'es) 129–30

113 fellingly/sellingly (? sellingly) 123, 126, 129
119 dosie/dazzie (dizzy) 123, 126, 129, 132
120 raw/yaw (yaw) 123, 126–9
132 doo't/too't (to't) 123, 126–9
159 reponsiue/responsiue (responsive) 124, 126, 129
167 it be/it be might (it might be) 124, 126–9
195 did sir/did so sir (did comply, sir,) 124, 129, 139
197 breede (bevy) 149
204 etc. Ostricke (Osric) 149
261 all (till) 138–9
283 Vnice/Onixe (union) 124, 127
307 against (gainst) 233
310 sure (afeard) 149
326 houres (hour of) 140
327 my hand (thy hand) 140
337 the Onixe (thy union) 127
356 shall I leaue (shall live) 141–2
394 for no (forc'd) 146
403 drawe no (draw on) 148

§ VII. THE INTERFERENCE OF THE PRESS-CORRECTOR

(*a*) Evidence of the corrector's presence

So far we have been considering the text of 1605 as the product of a harassed and ill-instructed compositor working from a difficult copy written and spelt by William Shakespeare. But, as we have already noted, the situation is really far more complicated than this. For years I lived in hopeful anticipation of finding nothing but compositors in the F1 *Hamlet* between us and the Globe prompt-book, and in Q2 between us and Shakespeare's manuscript. In both my hopes were disappointed upon closer examination by the unexpected discovery of fresh agents of corruption, an inattentive copyist for the press in the one case and in the other an active corrector. The corrector's hand is seen in the list of seventy-seven "Misprints not yet accounted for" with which the survey of Q2 concluded in the last section.

Not that his presence is a mere matter of inference. There is plenty of direct evidence for it, though Furness seems to be the only critic who has hitherto noticed it.[1] Six copies of Q2 are known of in the world, three in this country and three in the United States, each copy being in a different library. The three English copies are to be seen at the British Museum, at Trinity College Library, Cambridge (the "Capell" copy), and at the Bodleian (a copy on loan, belonging to Lord Grimston, Earl of Verulam). Those in America are in the Library of the Elizabethan Club, New Haven (the "Huth" copy), in the Henry Huntington Library (the "Devonshire" copy), and in the Folger Shakespeare Memorial Library, Washington. I have read five of these six copies, those at the British Museum, Trinity College Library and the Bodleian in the original, the "Huth" copy in photostat, and the "Devonshire" copy in the Griggs facsimile, the plates of which, it should be remarked, cannot always be relied upon for minutiae.[2] In these five copies there are no less than

[1] *Vide* Variorum *Hamlet*, II, p. 33, which gives a table of variants, based on the Ashbee facsimiles, and differing in certain details from my table below.

[2] It gives, for example, "fane" for "tane" at 5.2.245 which for long I took as a variant. Since I wrote the above Miss Henrietta Bartlett has been good enough to check the Folger copy with a list of variants I sent her, and it appears that it agrees closely with the Devonshire copy. Unfortunately I had not discovered the variants at 1.3.48,

eighteen clear cases of variant readings, apart from the two
already noted on pp. 93–4 which have nothing to do with
correction. These may be set out in the following table,
what I take as the uncorrected readings being given first:

Internal variants in the Second Quarto

Imprint	(inner O)	1604 (Dev., Huth, Folg.)
		1605 (B.M., Cap., Grim.)
1.1.107	(outer B)	Romeage (B.M., Grim.)
		Romadge (Cap., Dev., Huth., Folg.)
1.3. 48	(inner C)	step (Dev., Huth, B.M.)
		steepe (Cap., Grim.)
70	(inner C)	by (Dev., Huth, B.M.)
		buy (Cap., Grim.)
?1.4.69	(inner D)	my (Dev., Huth)
		my Lord (B.M., Cap., Grim.)[1]
2.2.617	(outer G)	braues (B.M.)
		braines (Cap., Dev., Huth, Grim., Folg.)
3.1.169	(outer G)	[*exit* omitted] (B.M.)
		exit, (Cap., Dev., Huth, Grim., Folg.)
5.1.321	(outer N)	thirtie (Dev., Huth, Folg.)
		thereby (B.M., Cap., Grim.)
5.2. 9	(outer N)	pall (Dev., Huth, Folg.)
		fall (B.M., Cap., Grim.)
113	(outer N)	sellingly (Dev., Huth, Folg., B.M.)
		fellingly (Cap., Grim.)
119	(outer N)	dosie (Dev., Huth, Folg.)
		dazzie (B.M., Cap., Grim.)
120	(outer N)	yaw (Dev., Huth, Folg.)
		raw (B.M., Cap., Grim.)
132	(outer N)	too't (Dev., Huth, Folg.)
		doo't (B.M., Cap., Grim.)

1.3.70, 1.4.69, 5.2.159 and in the printer's signature on the last page
when I consulted her.

[1] This is a doubtful instance, since the word "Lord" occurs at the
end of a long line and may therefore have been cut off by the edge
of the frisket like the letters noted on pp. 93–4.

159	(outer N)	reponsiue (Dev., Huth, B.M., ?Folg.)
		responsiue (Cap., Grim.)[1]
167	(outer N)	be hangers (Dev., Huth, Folg.)
		be might hangers (B.M., Cap., Grim.)
195	(outer N)	A did sir (Dev., Huth, Folg.)
		A did so sir (B.M., Cap., Grim.)
283	(inner N)	Vnice (Dev., Huth, Folg.)
		Onixe (B.M., Cap., Grim.)
Sig.	(inner O)	G. 2 (Dev., Huth, ?Folg.)
		O2 (Cap., Grim. [B.M.][2])

Variants in the same edition are not, of course, at all unusual in books of this period; and they arise, as is well known, through correction in the printer's forme, that is to say, the pages of type which when printed off represent one side of a sheet. And as such corrections are made during the actual progress of the printing, sheets both in the corrected and uncorrected state get sewn up together in the finished book. Nine variants of this kind are to be found, for example, in the Q1 of *Richard II* (1597), and it happens that each of the three extant copies of that text is unique. It follows that only by chance have the particular variants catalogued above been preserved in the six extant copies of *Hamlet* Q2. It should be remarked also that the two dates on the title-pages in no way indicate two different editions. All they imply is that the book was being printed about the turn of the year and that the compositor set up one date and the corrector preferred the other. But this correction is important from the point of view of text nomenclature: it means that Q2 was certainly not published until 1605 and that this date should therefore be given it in its modern descriptive title.

The striking feature about the list, of course, is that ten of the eighteen variants occur in act 5, seven of them being concerned with the difficult dialogue between Hamlet and

---

[1] I owe the detection of this variant to Mrs Murrie.
[2] This is inferential as B.M. lacks the last leaf.

Osric, most of which, as F1 shows, the Globe book-holder decided to dispense with. And as a matter of fact all ten belong to sheet N of the book, and nine of them to the outer forme [1] of that sheet. The last (Vnice/Onixe), however, comes from the inner forme, which shows that both formes were corrected. We are fortunate to have so many variants in a single forme, since we are thus enabled to watch the press-corrector at work and to see what are "corrections" and what are the original readings. Indeed, he gives himself away in the very first instance. The true reading of 5.1.321, as F1 shows, is:

> An houre of quiet shortly shall we see;

and it is obvious that, whether because Shakespeare happened here to form his "sh" like "th", or for some other reason, "shortlie" was set up as "thirtie" by the compositor, who thus produced the absurd line:

> An houre of quiet thirtie shall we see;

which the corrector altered to:

> An houre of quiet thereby shall we see,

and so made sense, though not at all the sense Shakespeare had intended. The example is instructive in more ways than one. It shows us

(i) that for the outer forme of sheet N, apart from

---

[1] It may perhaps be explained that the two formes represent the two sides of a sheet after printing and before being folded for sewing. In a quarto which has eight pages to a sheet, the pages are thus distributed in the formes: outer forme, pages 1, 4, 5, 8; inner forme, pages 2, 3, 6, 7. The reader unaccustomed to bibliographical notions may amuse himself by folding a square piece of paper in half and then in half again, so as to make four square leaves or eight pages, numbering the said pages and then opening out the sheet to its full extent, when he will find the numbers falling in the order set out above. Charles Sayle initiated me into this mystery at the University Library, Cambridge, about thirty years ago. It was he also who first explained to me the difference between a folio, a quarto, and an octavo.

two instances to be dealt with in a moment, the British Museum, Grimston and Capell copies give us the corrected sheet, while the other three copies preserve the original state;

(ii) that the corrector, as our experience of most other corrected books of the period would lead us to expect, has taken no trouble to consult Shakespeare's original copy;[1] and

(iii) that therefore none of the other variants belonging to outer sheet N in the British Museum, Grimston, and Capell copies are likely to possess any authority whatever.

This third point is an important editorial fact, inasmuch as at least two of these "corrections" are to be found in most modern texts, viz. "fellingly" (interpreted "feelingly"), and "doo't", while "raw" also finds its defenders from time to time. Yet, it may be categorically stated that, except for "thirtie" and the three passages with omissions at ll. 159, 167 and 195, the uncorrected readings in this forme are none of them in need of correction, though "dosie" is no doubt an old-fashioned spelling. As for the omissions, apart from the case of 'reponsiue', which at first escaped his eye, the corrector guessed wrong at l. 195, as F1 "He did Complie with his Dugge" indicates, though when confronted at l. 167 with the sentence "I would it be hangers till then" he could hardly help seeing that the word "might" had been omitted. He accordingly, we must

---

[1] Dr Greg informs me that in the quarto of *King Lear* printed by Nathaniel Butter in 1608 the corrector sometimes guessed and sometimes consulted the copy. I can find no definite evidence in *Hamlet* 1605 that Roberts' corrector did anything but guess. The insertion of "might" at 5.2.167 was demonstrably a shot though a successful one. And even the alteration of "braues" to "braines" at 2.2.617 would not be very difficult after a glance at the context. That "braines" and not "braues" was the corrector's word in this instance is I think clear from the other correction in forme outer G, seeing that the "*exit*" at 3.1.169 is far more likely to have been added by him than deleted once it was set up.

suppose, wrote it in the margin of the sheet and directed the compositor to insert it. The latter did so; and had to reset four lines of type to get it in. Nevertheless, after all this trouble, he actually introduced the word at the wrong place, so that the corrected sheet gives us "I would it be might hangers till then"! The point is eloquent of the kind of workmen we have to deal with.

The variant "Vnice"/Onixe" in the inner forme of sheet N is illuminating in a different fashion. Shakespeare's word, as we learn from F1 and Q1[1] was "Union", i.e. a large single pearl. This he probably wrote "Vniõ", a form which would explain the misprint "Vnice", since a careless curl over the "o" might give it the appearance of an "e", while if, as we have seen frequently happened, Shakespeare did not count his minim-strokes and wrote four instead of three minims for "ni", the combination might be misread as "nic". Anyhow, the corrector, finding "Vnice" in sheet N, would naturally alter it to "Onixe". Now the same jewel, as it happens, is mentioned again at 5.2.337, that is in the last half-sheet O which consists of $3\frac{1}{2}$ pages of type only[2]. And the point to notice is that here also it appears as "Onixe" in all six copies. This implies either of two things, (i) that this "Onixe" was likewise a correction, though no specimen containing "Vnice" has come down to us, or more probably (ii) that the last half-sheet was not set up or at least not printed until after the intervention of the corrector in inner N, which is what one would expect if a single compositor was at work upon the book.

The first of these alternatives, whether valid or not, raises considerations of great moment to an editor. As I have said, chance and chance alone determined that these

[1] Q1 gives "Vnion" at 5.2.337 only, but that suffices for the argument.

[2] Including the title page. I assume that this belonged to inner forme O because it is natural to suppose that the two sheet O corrections were made in the same forme.

particular eighteen variants should survive. They occur in seven different formes, i.e. outer B, inner C, inner D, outer G, outer N, inner N, and inner O. It is therefore possible that had all the original copies come down to us we should discover corrections in the other nineteen formes as well, though it is unlikely that any one of them would contain so many variants as outer N, which with its Osric dialogue was, no doubt, thought to be in a specially bad state.

Two trivial cases of such hypothetical correction may be traced with tolerable certainty. The "*Ham.*" speech-heading is found missing in all six copies at the head of a couple of Hamlet's speeches, the one at 3.2.61 and the other at 3.2.400. Both speeches begin at the top of the last page of a sheet, i.e. in outer G and outer H, and in both cases the heading is found correctly given in the catchword at the foot of the preceding page which falls in the inner forme. Dr McKerrow, who drew my attention to these absent speech-headings, also notes that the catchwords present a peculiar feature which requires explanation; the peculiarity in question being that, whereas in all the twenty-two other instances of speech-headings appearing as catchwords in this text they invariably stand alone, here they are given with the first word of the speech that follows. It is not difficult to see what happened. At first the compositor, omitting words in his usual fashion, overlooked the speech-headings altogether, and so set up not only the opening lines of sig. G 4v and sig. H 4v without their speech-headings, but also employed the first words of the speeches as catchwords instead of the abbreviated *Ham.* In due course the corrector, perceiving the omission,[1] ordered its rectification; and the addition of the speech-headings to the catchwords is evidence that the compositor carried out

---

[1] It was not necessary for him to consult the copy to do this; the final speeches in sig. G 4R and H 4R are very brief, and it requires no intelligence to see that they must be followed by the other speaker of the duologue.

the orders as far as the inner formes were concerned. But the speeches themselves belong to the outer formes, which had apparently been printed before the inner formes were taken in hand and had in fact been completed when the corrector intervened, so that it was too late to do anything about the prefixes at the head of sigs. G 4v and H 4v.

Furthermore, forme outer N presents a clear case of double correction. It will have been noticed that, whereas in this forme seven of the corrections are found in the B.M., Capell, and Grimston copies, two of them, "fellingly" and "responsiue" occur in Capell and Grimston only, a state of affairs which makes it certain that the forme was twice corrected, so that we have copies in three different states. First of all there was the printing which produced the uncorrected state (State A), in the Devonshire, Huth and Folger copies. Next, seven corrections were made (Corr. I), "thereby", "fall", "dazzie", "raw", "doo't", "be might hangers", "A did so sir", which produced State B in which the B.M. copy was printed. Next, two further corrections were made (Corr. II), "fellingly" and "responsiue", which produced State C in which the Capell and Grimston copies were printed. There is nothing surprising in this. Double correction in the same forme is to be found in other books of the period; and Dr Greg, with whose help I have been able to work out this particular problem, finds a similar case in the Pied Bull Quarto of *King Lear*.

Once again, what certainly happened in outer forme N may have occurred in other formes also. Take, for instance, 5.2.43 from the inner forme of sheet N, a forme we can prove to have been corrected, since it contains the variant "Vnice/Onixe". In F1 the line runs:

And many such like Assis of great charge,

the word "Assis" being a quibble upon "asses" and the plural of "as" the conjunction. Now it seems that Shakespeare, as not infrequently happened, wrote the final "s" of the word in such a way that it might be read "r",[1] for the line in Q2 appears:

> And many such like, as sir of great charge.

Yet the intrusive comma and the divided word tell us that more than mere misreading is here involved. Shakespeare's "assis" might have been misread "assir" but could not possibly have been mistaken for "as sir" because that would give "as" a final "s" which is, of course, of totally different formation from an initial or medial "s" in the handwriting of that time. It follows, therefore, that the compositor first set up "aſsir",[2] and that this was afterwards corrected by simple division and transposition of letters to "as ſir" and a comma inserted to make all well. But "such like, as sir" is found in all six copies of the text, i.e. it occurs like "Onixe" of sheet O in both a corrected and an uncorrected forme. We are thus forced to conclude that the correction was made on a different occasion from that to which the correction in the list of variants belongs.

It is of course possible that in this case the two corrections belong to different processes; in other words, that the change from "aſsir" to "as ſir" was made in proof, and not while the sheets were actually being printed off, as "Vnice/Onixe" must have been. This would agree with what we know of the compositor and what we may suspect about his relations with the press-corrector, who if he did not trust his man would be likely to scrutinise the proofs carefully and then check his work again during the printing. Assuming such a condition of affairs, it would follow that we have to reckon not only with the eighteen certain corrections cited above and other possible corrections during the final printing of which variants do not happen to have

---

[1] Cf. "the vmber" for "thumbes" (3.2.373) discussed in vol. II, pp. 323–4 below.

[2] As often as not in this text medial double "s" is set up "ſs" rather than "ſſ".

survived, but also with corrections made in proof, of which
in the nature of the case we can have no direct evidence.
Moreover, the compositor being an indifferent workman,
the number of proof-corrections is likely to have been considerably greater than those made later. As is shown in the
list on pp. 120–1 we have sixty-two misprints in Q2 not
yet accounted for apart from fifteen items which we now
know for certain to have been corrections. Taking everything into consideration, I do not think it exceeds the limits
of probability to suppose that most of these sixty-two were
"corrections" made in proof, and we might even allow
ourselves a wider margin. On the other hand, each conjectural proof-correction must be discussed individually and
the conjecture shown to be reasonable before it can claim
a hearing. And this means, in the first place, that we must
study the methods of the press-corrector in the indisputable
readings for which he is responsible before venturing to
speculate upon the possibilities of his interference with the
text elsewhere.

A perusal of the list of certain corrections, or miscorrections as most of them should more properly be called,
on pp. 123–4 shows that they divide themselves into five
classes: (i) mere adjustments of spelling, such as "Romadge"
for "Romeage"; (ii) attempts to supply omitted letters,
e.g. "steepe" for "step", "buy" for "by", "responsiue"
for "reponsiue"; (iii) attempts to supply omitted words, e.g.
"be might hangers" for "be hangers" and "A did so sir"
for "A did sir"; (iv) miscorrections of misprinted words,
e.g. "thereby" for "thirtie" (shortlie), and "Onixe" for
"Vnice" (Vniδ); and (v) miscorrections arising from misunderstanding of Shakespeare's meaning, e.g. "fall" for
"pall", "fellingly" for "sellingly", "dazzie" for "dosie",
"raw" for "yaw", and "doo't" for "too't".

The first of these classes we need not trouble much about.
Its chief interest is that it shows us the corrector touching
up Shakespeare's spelling, for such I take "Romeage" to

be. Moreover, even if Q2 contained a large number of instances belonging to it, they would be difficult if not impossible to detect unless variants happened to survive, as one has at 1.1.107. The possibility should not, however, be overlooked of words strangely spelt by Shakespeare being mistaken for other words. This, for example, is I believe the explanation of the substitution of "dazzie" for "dosie". "Dosie" is an old-fashioned spelling of an unusual verb "dizzy" (*vide N.E.D.* "dozy"), and it looks as if the press-corrector may have altered it in the margin to "dazzle", a word the compositor in his turn misread "dazzie", which is of course sheer nonsense. The miscorrections of the second and third class are likely to be fairly numerous, since the corrector would soon grow aware of the compositor's propensity to miss out letters and words and be on his guard against it; at times too much on his guard, for there can be little doubt that he now and then discovered omissions that were not there. Those of the third class ought also to be easy to recognise, inasmuch as there being no clue to the lost word beyond the general context the corrector could only take a shot which would of course be generally wide of the mark.

As for the fourth and fifth classes, they may be considered as one from the corrector's point of view, seeing that he would not alter words unless he took them to be compositor's misprints. Furthermore—an important point—his alterations would be made on a quite different principle from that which guided the playhouse scribes in the F1 text. He would, for example, be most unlikely to perpetrate an emendation such as that which produced "Lunacies" for "browes" at 3.3.7 in F1, since he would know that no compositor, seeing the former word in his copy, could possibly set it up as the latter. At the same time, he was dominated by typographical considerations rather than graphical ones; and, if we may judge from the examples in our list, tended to attribute the errors of the compositor to inexperience with the type-case. Thus he alters "yaw" to "raw" and "pall" to "fall", though the letters "y" and "r", "p" and "f" have not the remotest resemblance to each other in the English script of the age. He simply assumed that the compositor had inadvertently set up the wrong letter, and emended accordingly.

Yet, though he emended, with no reference as far as I can discover to the original copy and with no guide but his own intelligence, his emendations are not entirely wanton. Like the F1 scribes he studied the context to some extent. He could not fail to see that an "s" was missing in 5.2.159 and the word "might" at 5.2.167; he scored successfully, if hardly brilliantly, with "steepe" and "buy"; he saw that "braines" was the right word at 2.2.617; he perceived that some kind of jewel lay behind the strange word "Vnice" and that "thereby" would make sense in 5.1.321. But unlike the F1 scribes he studied also the typographical form of the word he found it necessary to change; an alternative word of completely different form which appeared to give the sense required did not content him; and his main principle was economy of alteration. In four of the eight examples in our list belonging to classes (iv) and (v) he changed the initial letter only; "braues" and "braines" are very close to each other; while even in the pairs "thereby" and "thirtie", "dazzie" and "dosie", "Onixe" and "Vnice", the general framework is the same. In short, though the corrector is over-impetuous, that is to say over-impatient with the compositor, though he is stupid and almost always wrong, he has a conscience of a sort. Above all, we can feel some confidence that whatever word he substituted for the misprint, or supposed misprint, in the sheet before him, and however much he might fly in the face of graphical possibilities, the emendation would resemble the typographical structure of the misprint as closely as he could make it. And this confidence, for which I think our list of miscorrections gives full warrant, though no

compensation for what we have lost through his interference with the "simple fool" at the type-case, will at
any rate prove some guide in our speculations concerning
his misdeeds in those parts of Q2 where we cannot check
him by his own variants, speculations to which we may
now turn.

In other words, I now propose to consider a number of
misprints which may, I think, be reasonably regarded as
miscorrections, whether in proof or in the forme, belonging
to one or other of the five classes above described or to
classes nearly related to them. But before actually tackling
them, there is one last introductory point to be made; the
corrector might write his instructions in the margin of the
sheets, but he could not ensure that the compositor would
carry them out intelligently. The misplaced "might" in the
corrected forme at 5.2.167 proves that; and we shall do
well to be on the look out for other instances.

(b) Possibilities of correction elsewhere

In attempting to distinguish between compositor's errors
and his corrector's miscarriages, as in the attempt to
separate the work of the two scribes in F1, I am embarking
upon a hazardous undertaking, and one in which certainty
is out of the question. All I can hope to accomplish is to
show that out of the whole body of misprints in Q2 there
are some which are more likely to be miscorrections than
others. No harm can come of such an enquiry, since
provided a given reading is demonstrably wrong, or at least
clearly less Shakespearian than its parallel in the F1, it
matters little to an editor whether it be labelled misprint
or miscorrection. On the other hand, the enquiry may
bring definite gain, if it turns out that a certain number of
these readings cannot possibly or reasonably be ascribed to
the unaided genius of either compositor or corrector; for

we shall then be forced to probe deeper and discover, if we can, some further cause of textual disease. I shall not endeavour in what follows, be it observed, to prove a case, but merely to estimate possibilities. We *know* that we have in the text of 1605 a compositor and a corrector to deal with, and so far we know nothing more for certain. Are these known factors of corruption sufficient to explain all the aberrations of that text, or must we seek for some hitherto unsuspected factor? That is the chief question at issue.

The difficulty of distinguishing between the compositor and the corrector comes out at once when, following the fiye classes of miscorrections set forth above, we proceed to discuss which of the Q2 misprints should be allocated to the first class, that of *Adjustments of Spelling*. We have seen, for instance, on p. 105 that the misprints "reueale" (revel) and "leaue" (live) probably arose from a misunderstanding of the copy-spellings "reuele" and "leue", but this supposition does not help us to decide whether the compositor or the corrector deserves the honour of committing them. All we can say is that the inattention to the context displayed in both cases suggests the former rather than the latter, though it would be risky to suppose that the corrector always consulted his contexts before making changes, or that the compositor never did. Again, the form "abraode" at 1.1.161 looks like a miscorrection of "abrode" (a spelling found in other good quartos) with the "a" inserted in the wrong place. But the occurrence of "braod" at 3.3.81 and 3.4.2 raises the question whether both forms are not just spellings of the compositor himself.

Three misprints at least can, however, with fair probability be accounted for as miscorrected spellings. The first is "seale slaughter" for "selfe-slaughter" (1.2.132), which may be explained on the supposition that the Shakespearian spelling "sealfe" was set up in type, was marked for correction, and that then the "f" was inadvertently abstracted from the forme instead of the "a". The second, "addission"

(2.1.47), is even simpler; the spellings "Apparision" (1.2.211) and "innouasion" (2.2.347) suggest that "addision" was a possible form with Shakespeare; and the intrusive "t" was probably intended by the corrector to replace the "s". The third example furnishes, I believe, a miscorrection not of Shakespeare's spelling but of the compositor's, which we have seen reason to think included such forms as "well" for "will", and "tell" for "till".[1] Speaking of the intended eavesdropping behind the arras, Claudius says at 3.1.32–4, according to Q2:

> her father and my selfe,
> Wee'le so bestow our selues, that seeing vnseene,
> We may of their encounter franckly iudge.

Here F1 prints "Will" for "Wee'le", a much easier reading, and one the more likely to be genuine inasmuch as if the compositor set up "Well" instead of "Will" the corrector would naturally enough alter it to "Wee'le".

Attempts to Supply Omitted Letters are, in the nature of the case, even more difficult to detect than corrections of the first class. Where they are true corrections they pass of course out of the range of conjecture, unless variants happen to have survived as with "steepe/step" and "buy/by". The corrector, however, must have been on the alert for cases of the kind, and is likely therefore occasionally to have been led into miscorrection by this particular anxiety. I suggest, for instance, that the strange misprint "coold mother" for "good mother" at 1.2.77 may have arisen in this fashion. Here, I conjecture, the compositor, perhaps under the influence of the initial letter of the preceding word "cloake", accidentally set up "cood mother", which the corrector, supposing him to have omitted a letter, took as "coold (= cold) mother"—an

[1] *Vide* p. 113.

unusual criticism of Gertrude's character! At 1.3.75 again we have—

> Neither a borrower nor a lender boy,

for

> Neither a borrower nor a lender be,

where I explain "boy" as a miscorrection of a "literal" or $o:e$ misprint "bo" (be). Here, too, as belonging to the same forme we may consider the variant at 1.3.83:

> (F1) The time *inuites* you, goe, your seruants tend.
> (Q2) The time *inuests* you goe, your seruants tend.

Most editors read "invites", but "invests" has had its champions, among them Theobald, who declared that "invites you" had been substituted by the players for "invests you", which he explained as "besieges, presses upon you from every side". It sounds, indeed, far-fetched enough for Polonius; and I have myself played with the idea that it might be the true reading.[1] Second thoughts, however, persuade me that it cannot be so, inasmuch as "the time invites you" (cf. *Cymb.* 3.4.108, "The time inviting thee") is completely and convincingly Shakespearian. The "inuests" therefore must have arisen from some compositor's slip or (on the analogy of "well/will") compositor's spelling like "inuets", to which the corrector attempted to lend an air of plausibility by adding a supposititious missing letter. Still more plausible, if we had nothing but the Q2 text to go upon, would be "drownes" for "douts" at 4.7.192. And yet it is easy enough to guess the origin of the variant. Misreading a Shakespearian spelling like "dowts", the compositor set it up as "dowes" or as "downes" ($e:t$ and minim misreadings), and the corrector, noting the talk of drowning in the context, imagined that an "r" had been omitted.

On the other hand, Q2 presents us with at least three

---

[1] *Vide* the Cranach *Hamlet* (notes and p. 178).

instances, unless I am much mistaken, of the corrector
falling into the opposite error and mistaking what is really
a misprint by omission of a letter for one of another type.
There is, for example, the misprint "but" for "lust" at
1.5.55, which is due to nothing but the chance
omission of "s", the resultant "lut" being in turn naturally
corrected to "but". Or take the following variants from
3.2.407:

(F1) When Churchyards yawne, and Hell it selfe *breaths* out
Contagion to this world.
(Q2) When Churchyards yawne, and hell it selfe *breakes* out
Contagion to this world.

If Shakespeare wrote "breathes", as he is likely to have
done, and the Q2 compositor omitted the "t" in setting it
up, the result would be "breahes", which would immediately suggest a "literal" misprint of "breakes" to anyone
who knew the ways of compositors. With another misprint
by missing letter the corrector seems to have dealt differently.
"And an act hath three branches, it is to act, to do and to
perform; argall, she drowned herself wittingly", argues the
legally minded Grave-digger at 5.1.13. The quarto prints
the latter part of this "to doe, to performe, or all; she
drownd her selfe wittingly"; and we hardly need to conjecture what has happened, the whole business is so patent.
First the compositor has misread "argall", a word probably
new to him, as "orgall", then he has set it up without its
"g" through inadvertence, and last of all the corrector has
come along and transferred the semi-colon from one side
of the word to the other in the interest of what he takes to
be the meaning of the passage.

Two strange misprints, "and" for "bird" (1.5.116) and
"all" for "till" (5.2.261), I suspect also belong to this
class; for in the first instance the corrector seeing "come,
ird come" or "come, ind come" in the proof or in the
printed sheet, would naturally take the middle word as a

misprint of "and"; while in the second instance "but ill that time" would even more naturally be corrected to "but all that time".

The foregoing reconstructions of the corrector's little efforts are, of course, highly conjectural. In passing to the class of *Attempts to Supply Omitted Words*, we are on surer ground. Indeed, it is possible to give a list of seven misprints which are almost certainly errors of this kind, as may be seen at a glance when the F1 readings are compared with those of Q2. In order to make the matter clearer still, I head the list with one of the two miscorrected omissions of which we can be absolutely certain:

5.2.195

(F1) He did *Complie* with his Dugge[1]
(Q2 uncor.) A did sir with his dugge
(,, cor.) A did *so* sir with his dugge

1.2.175

(F1) Wee'l teach you to drinke *deepe*, ere you depart.
(Q2) Weele teach you *for* to drinke ere you depart.

1.3.77

(F1) And borrowing *duls the* edge of Husbandry.
(Q2) And borrowing *dulleth* edge of husbandry.

2.2.43[2]

(F1) Haue I, my Lord? Assure *you*, my good Liege
(Q2) Haue I my Lord? *I* assure my good Liege

3.2.200

(F1) Which now *like* Fruite vnripe stickes on the Tree
(Q2) Which now *the* fruite vnripe sticks on the tree

---

[1] It will be noticed that F1 also has its omission in this passage, which in an edited text should read:

"A' did comply, sir, with his dug".

[2] *Vide* pp. 162–3 for a discussion of this.

4.5.160

(F1) Oh Heauens, is't possible, a yong Maids wits,
      Should be as mortall as an *old* mans life?
(Q2) O heauens, ist possible a young maids wits
      Should be as mortall as a *poore* mans life.

5.1.252

(F1) She should in ground vnsanctified *haue* lodg'd
(Q2) She should in ground vnsanctified *been* lodg'd†

5.1.260[1]

(F1) To sing *sage* Requiem, and such rest to her
(Q2) To sing *a* Requiem and such rest to her

And to these I should be inclined to add, with scarcely less
hesitation:

5.1.270

(F1) Oh treble woe,[2]
      Fall ten times *trebble*, on that cursed head
(Q2) O treble woe[3]
      Fall tenne times *double* on that cursed head

5.2.326

(F1) In thee, there is not halfe an *houre of* life
(Q2) In thee there is not halfe an *houres* life

The following, on the other hand, may belong to this class
or may be simply a compositor's careless substitution of one
pronoun for another:

5.2.327

(F1) The Treacherous Instrument is in *thy* hand.
(Q2) The treacherous instrument is in *my* hand.

I quote it here because if, as we have just seen, the corrector
was probably fiddling with the line before, he may well
have been responsible for this variant also.

The foregoing examples suggest that the corrector in

---

[1] *Vide* p. 11.   [2] F1 misprints this "Oh terrible woer".
[3] These three words occur at the foot of a page and what follows
at the head of the next, a fact which helps to account for the error.

making his alterations was guided not only by the sense of the context but by the metre also; and the opening lines of the Gonzago play seem to offer an amusing instance of his being misled by similar considerations into assuming an omission which was not actually there. The lines (3.2.165–6) are correctly given in F1:

> Full thirtie times hath Phoebus Cart gon round,
> Neptunes salt Wash, and Tellus *Orbed* ground.

But the second of them appears in Q2 as

> Neptunes salt wash, and Tellus *orb'd the* ground,

and the explanation is, I conjecture, that the compositor set up "orb'd" instead of "orbed", and that the corrector, taking it for a finite verb with "Tellus" as the subject, and perceiving the defective metre, added a "the" to supply what he imagined was an omission.

Another example of the same species is, I think, to be found at 5.2.355–6, which Q2 prints

> O god Horatio, what a wounded name,
> Things standing thus vnknowne, shall I leaue behind me?

and F1

> Oh good Horatio, what a wounded name,
> (Things standing thus vnknowne) shall liue behind me.

Jennens alone among editors has followed Q2 in the second line, and he is never likely to gain adherents, since the F1 reading is manifestly superior both in metre and diction. Moreover, the misprint "leaue" for "liue" at 3.4.158 in Q2 gives us the clue to this later corruption. The explanation, we have seen,[1] of that misprint is that Shakespeare employed the not uncommon spelling "leue" for "liue", a spelling however which was unfortunately also current for "leaue". But whereas

> And leaue the purer with the other halfe

[1] *Vide* p. 105.

makes a sort of sense which might pass muster with the corrector, a phrase like "shall leaue behind me" calls out for adjustment, and the insertion of "I" would almost inevitably follow on the supposition that the compositor, as usual, had omitted a word. A curious feature of this case is that the variant reading in Q1, which runs

> O fie Horatio, and if thou shouldst die,
> What a scandale wouldst thou leaue behinde?—

seems to suggest that the word "leave" passed into the prompt-book and was spoken on the stage. The evidence of F1 is, however, against this; and I can only suppose that the coincidence is an accidental one, due perhaps to mishearing on the part of the pirate, "live" and "leave" being closer phonologically in the sixteenth century than they are now.

The foregoing miscorrection shows that the corrector's ear for blank verse was not an impeccable one; and the next two Q2 variants, if we may assign them to his hand, are possibly attempts to restore the sense without realisation that the metre has suffered through the omission of a monosyllable:

1.2.137

(F1) That it should come *to this*
(Q2) that it should come *thus*[1]

2.2.587

(F1) Had he the Motiue and *the Cue* for passion
(Q2) Had he the motiue, and *that* for passion

And with these may be included a similar adjustment of the sense, though this time in prose. "What meanes your Lordship?" enquires Ophelia at 3.1.106 (F1); to which Hamlet replies, "That if you be honest and faire, your Honesty should admit no discourse to your Beautie". The word

---

[1] On the other hand the compositor may be solely responsible, since he confuses "this" and "thus" elsewhere, i.e. at 5.1.308. Cf. p. 107.

"honesty" has vanished from the Q2 text, probably through inadvertence, but advertence has been at work also, as is seen by the change of "your" to "you" in order to make sense.

Under the head of miscorrected omissions too should, I think, be grouped a curious trio of misprints, which look at first sight like those compositor's anticipations spoken of on p. 54, two of them having already been there touched upon. They are:

1.2.67

(F1) Not so my Lord, I am too much i'th'Sun.
(Q2) Not so much my Lord, I am too much in the sonne.

2.2.566-7

(F1) a speech of some dosen or sixteene lines
(Q2) a speech of some dosen lines, or sixteene lines

3.2.233

(F1) If once a Widdow, euer I be Wife.
(Q2) If once I be a widdow, euer I be a wife.

I connect these printer's vagaries with the misplaced "might" at 5.2.167, and suggest that we have here to deal with double correction. In other words, taking 1.2.67 as an illustration, my hypothesis is that first of all the compositor omitted "much"; then, under instruction from the corrector inserted it, but at the wrong place; and lastly, a second time under correction, set the word up once again, this time at the right spot, neglecting however, as he did so, to abstract the word he had originally inserted. This may or may not be an exact account of what happened; and the third example must be even more complicated and involve perhaps double omission as well as double correction. In any event, I think we ought to feel pretty safe in assigning omission and miscorrection as the general cause for all three, as it almost certainly is for the transposed "to refraine night" at 3.4.165, which is a close parallel to "I would it be might hangers".

We have now reached the fourth class of *Miscorrections of Misprinted Words*, i.e. those committed with the intention of rectifying compositors' slips or misreadings. A good example of the former is the half-corrected "cull-cold maydes" (F1, "cold Maids") at 4.7.172, where the original misprint "cull" (? a shot at "could") remains in the Q2 text. Or take the transformation of the couplet at the end of 4.3—

> (F1) And thou must cure me: Till I know 'tis done,
>   How ere my happes, my ioyes were ne're begun

into

> (Q2) And thou must cure me: till I know tis done,
>   How ere my haps, my ioyes will nere begin.

This can, perhaps, best be explained by imagining that the compositor first set up "will nere begun" by one of those accidental changes of verb to which all compositors are prone, and that the corrector then corrected his grammar. A slip again like "in" for "is" is one of which almost any compositor may at times be guilty. When therefore 1.3.3—

> And convoy is assistant, do not sleep

becomes

> And conuay, in assistant doe not sleepe

in Q2, it is not difficult to guess that the corrector has shifted the position of the comma in an attempt to make sense of a doubly misprinted line. We suspected him, it will be remembered, of shifting a semi-colon at 5.1.13 for the same purpose. In a word, the phenomenon of miscorrection is as germane to the subject of punctuation as it is to that of readings in general.

As for the correction of misreadings, Shakespeare's handwriting must, I fancy, have been partly responsible for the following group of misprints.

> Now might I doe it, but now a is a praying

is what Q2 gives us at 3.3.73; and the line might have stood unchallenged in all modern editions, had not F1 printed the variant—

Now might I do it pat, now he is praying,

which proves beyond cavil that Shakespeare wrote "pat" not "but". Yet the Q2 reading strongly suggests that he wrote it in such a way that it looked like "put", since if the compositor so set it up his corrector would naturally assume that the "p" was a turned "b".† The misprint is then in the nature of a minim-misreading,[1] as also, if I am not mistaken, is "they yawne" for "they aime" at 4.5.9. The word "aime" with its four minim-strokes might easily be misread as "awne"; and if so set up, would then present the corrector with something which he might as easily take for "yawne", on the supposition that an initial letter had been omitted.

It is clear that Shakespeare occasionally wrote "l" or "t" in a way which rendered it liable to confusion with "k", a letter at this period formed after a manner not very dissimilar, in careless script, from those just mentioned. There is, for instance, a striking *l:k* misprint or mistranscription in F1, viz. "to take" for "totall" (2.2.479). It is not therefore surprising to find the same kind of misprint in Q2. That of "kyth" for "tythe" (3.4.97) and "Worke" for "Would" (4.7.20), have already been noted,[2] a pair which, unlike as they seem in type, might in a careless Elizabethan hand be mistaken letter by letter for each other. All which, however, is but preliminary to a consideration of the interesting variant at 2.2.468:

(F1) One Speech[3] in it, I cheefely lou'd, 'twas Æneas *Tale* to Dido
(Q2) one speech in't I chiefely loued, t'was Aeneas *talke* to Dido

The second of these readings, it has actually been claimed, "may well have been the author's first shot".[4] It is there-

---

[1] *Vide* pp. 108–9.   [2] *Vide* p. 111.
[3] F1 prints "cheefe Speech", cf. p. 55.
[4] Greg, *Emendation*, p. 57; *Aspects*, p. 184.

fore important to point out that it is quite naturally explained as "tale" misprinted "take" and then miscorrected to "talke".

Finally, the quite ingenious correction at 5.2.394, which gives us instead of

Of deaths put on by cunning and forc'd cause

the Q2 reading

Of deaths put on by cunning, and for no cause,

was probably helped a little by Shakespeare's handwriting in which "rcd" might resemble "rno" if carelessly penned.

A characteristic of most of the foregoing corrections is the superficial speciousness of the corrector's readings, a quality they share with the "raw", "doo't", and "fellingly" of outer forme N, which have beguiled so many modern editors. We have seen that a case can be made for "inuests" (1.3.83); and the "but" at 3.3.73 and "drownes" at 4.7.192 seem to make excellent sense until we turn to the F1 variants, while "for no cause" (5.2.394) and "Aeneas talke to Dido" (2.2.468) might both be defended as conceivably Shakespearian. Even "they yawne at it" (4.5.9)[1] and "hell it selfe breakes out Contagion" (3.2.407), odd as they appear at first blush, would no doubt pass muster with editors had they no F1 text. The corrector was more knowing than the compositor; as I have said, he studied his contexts as he went to work, and there is generally an idea of some kind behind his alterations. It follows that in dealing with our fifth class of *Miscorrections due to Misunderstanding*, i.e. those which are virtually emendations due to misapprehension of Shakespeare's meaning, we must

---

[1] It is surprising that this has apparently found no defenders, since "yawn" means "gape" and is more than once used by Shakespeare to mean "gape with wonder or amazement" (cf. *Cor.* 3.2.11, *Oth.* 5.2.101).

proceed with added caution. Some of them are, of course, absurd on the face of it; while the plausibility of others yields to scrutiny. But there are others again which have to be weighed most carefully before they are rejected. For it should never be forgotten that Q2 is the better text of the two at our disposal, and that we need a very strong case before we dismiss any of its readings in favour of alternatives from a text twice transcribed and unscrupulously man-handled in the process. Ultimately, too, those reasons must be aesthetic ones, for which the critic has to draw upon his own taste and judgment. For however elaborate be our critical apparatus, no apparatus by itself can edit Shake-speare.

Furthermore, the line between miscorrections of this class and the group of Q2 misprints, considered in detail on pp. 106–13, which may be regarded as misreadings of Shakespeare's handwriting, is a shadowy one; and it may well be that a fair proportion of the latter class should be transferred to the former. Certainly, if we can take the number of corrections in sheet N as a guide to what happened in other sheets, the proportion belonging to the category of misunderstanding is a very high one. The principle I have, however, found it simplest to adopt for the present purpose is to assume that a misprint of this type is a compositor's misreading unless it possesses features that suggest miscorrection. The chief reason for the difficulty in distinguishing between these two species of misprint is the probability, already noted, that the corrector was careful to interfere as little as possible with the type-letters of the word he was altering, and though he paid little regard to graphical considerations his economy of change would inevitably often result in emendations which might be taken as misreadings of the F1 variant.

Let us begin, however, by looking at examples which we can more or less confidently assign to miscorrection, because as in the case of the change from "pall" to "fall", graphical confusion is out of the question. A good instance to take first is that seen in the following variants at 2.2.232–3:

(F1) Happy, in that we are not ouer-happy: on Fortunes Cap, we are not the very Button.

(Q2) Happy, in that we are not euer happy on Fortunes lap, We are not the very button.

A little knowledge is a dangerous thing, especially in the printing-house. Everyone knows "the lap of Fortune"; but who has ever heard of "Fortune's cap"? Moreover if, as seems likely, the "euer" for "ouer" is a misprint on the compositor's part, that would assist the misunderstanding, seeing that "on Fortune's lap" a person would naturally be "euer happy". The corrector had an almost overwhelming case, he would think, for changing the "c" to an "l". And having done so, it should be observed, he emended the punctuation to suit. Contrariwise, had he perceived that there was something wrong with the punctuation at 3.1.150–2, though it was only the omission of a comma, he might not have found it necessary to make the correction evident in "you gig & amble, and you list you nickname Gods creatures", which is what Q2 reads for "you gig, you amble and you lisp, you nickname Gods creatures".[1] It is he too, we may guess, who "corrected", this time in the best social sense, the rude Clown's "intill" at 5.1.81 to the more polite "into"; while another change (5.2.403) which belongs, I think, without doubt to him, is that which instead of

And from his mouth, whose voyce will draw on more

gives us

And from his mouth, whose voyce will drawe no more.

Inspired as it clearly is by the notion that the voice like the breath could not be drawn in death, it furnishes a measure of the corrector's intelligence. But the most precious

---

[1] *Vide* vol. II, p. 281 for this, which I take as the true reading.

example of his interference is, I suggest, the spelling "Ostricke" for "Osric" or "Osricke" throughout the whole of sheet N; and that the error is his and not the compositor's is, I think, strongly suggested by the fact that the name appears correctly spelt in a stage-direction and speech-heading of sheet O (5.2.361). But why this change of spelling, which makes the fop look like a kind of bird? I believe the answer is that the corrector, studying his context as usual, and perceiving talk of a "Lapwing" with a "shell on his head" (5.2.193) a few lines before the name first appears in the text (5.2.204), actually imagined that the author intended to give him a bird-like name. And if all this be so, it is still further evidence for double correction in sheet N, the sheet in which most of our certain corrections occur.

It remains to glance at a group of readings in Q2 which though clearly inferior, or so they seem to me, to their F1 variants, possess like the Misreadings quoted on pp. 106–13, close graphical similarity to them, together with what I have called above the same typographical framework, and also, I should suppose, enough appropriateness to their context to satisfy a working printer. Here are fourteen examples, one or two of which have already been commented on, their F1 variants being given in brackets:

*1.1. 73 cost (Cast)	3.1. 72 despiz'd (dispriz'd)
*1.4. 49 interr'd (enurn'd)	3.1.160 expectation (expectansie)
1.5. 20 fearefull (fretfull)	4.7. 7 criminall (crimefull)
*1.5. 33 rootes (rots)	4.7. 20 Worke (Would)
1.5. 95 swiftly (stiffely)	*5.1.286 wisedome (wisenesse)
2.2.381 mouths (mowes)	5.2.197 breede (Beauy)
2.2.450 friendly (French)	5.2.310 sure (affear'd)

* *Vide* p. 152.

Allowing for small varieties of spelling, such as "inurn'd" instead of "enurn'd", or "beauie" instead of "beauy", and for obvious graphical affinities, such as "f" and long "s", "h" and "y", "e" and "d", of which any contemporary printer would be aware, each of these fourteen readings appears open to three alternative explanations. Either (i) the compositor, unable to read Shakespeare's word, set up some nonsense which the corrector translated into sense as best he could, or (ii) the corrector found the word that Shakespeare intended in type, but misunderstood it and therefore emended it, or (iii) the compositor, baffled by Shakespeare's handwriting, himself emended by setting up a word similar in graphical outline to that he was trying to decipher and at the same time more or less suitable to the context. For, as we have already suggested, the compositor did not necessarily always make nonsense when he could not read a word; not being entirely inhuman, he too would take his shots. In a word, the fourteen Q2 variants seem to belong to an indeterminate group which may be labelled misreadings or miscorrections with equal probability. It is unnecessary here to discuss each item separately; a general inspection of the list as a whole should suffice to bring out its significance. And it is interesting to observe that a similar list of variants which are best explained as either misreadings or miscorrections, this time by one or other of the transcribers, can be compiled from F1. Eighteen examples of the kind may be quoted, and it will be seen how close is the graphical resemblance between the variants in every case, due allowance being made for Elizabethan script:

1.1. 98	Landlesse (lawelesse)	3.1. 86	pith (pitch)
1.1.163	talkes (takes)	3.1. 87	turne away (turne awry)
1.2.243	wake (walke)	3.2. 65	like (licke)[3]
1.5. 71	bak'd (barckt)[1]	3.2. 67	faining (fauning)
2.2. 12	humour (hauior)	3.2.351	freely (surely)
2.2.137	winking (working)[2]	3.4.182	blunt (blowt)
2.2.142	Precepts (prescripts)	3.4.188	made (mad)
2.2.524	O who (a woe)	4.4. 8	safely (softly)
2.2.616	Scullion (stallyon)	4.7. 96	mad (made)

[1] Cf. pp. 59–60.   [2] Cf. pp. 74–5.
[3] Cf. "Warlicke" (warlike), 4.6.15.

I have been at pains to go into the question of mis-correction rather thoroughly, because a good deal depends upon it, more than appears at first sight. Our main purpose throughout this enquiry is to recover Shakespeare's manu-script of *Hamlet*; and now we feel confident that it lies behind the Q2 text, the only means of recovery or restora-tion is to peel off, as it were, the dirt left upon its surface by the craftsmen who last had sight of it and were responsible for its perpetuation in printer's type. For Q2, like the F1 text, is subject to a double process of corruption, one layer of dirt above the other; and that we are now able to look at the manuscript through the eyes of the compositor has only become possible because we are at last in a position, if not to push the corrector altogether aside, at least to esti-mate the possibilities of his well-intentioned but unhappy interference.

CHAPTER IV

Shakespeare and the Globe

§VIII. DID SHAKESPEARE HANDLE THE PROMPT-BOOK?

(*a*) Dr Greg's theory of "first shots" and "second thoughts"

But there is another and equally important purpose behind the foregoing lengthy and, I fear, over-speculative disquisition. It was undertaken in the first instance, it will be remembered, in order to discover whether we had got to the bottom of the corruption in the Q2 of 1605. Can we be certain that the compositor and the corrector are the only sources of that corruption? Or is there some other possible explanation of readings in Q2 which make good sense and are yet apparently of inferior authority to their parallels in F1, readings which constitute a fair proportion of the list on p. 149? That these are no idle questions is proved by the four readings in the list which I have marked with an asterisk. For "cost", "interr'd", "rootes" and "wisedom" are to be found not only in Q2 but also in Q1; and Q1, as we have assumed, represents a report of performances of *Hamlet* on the stage at the beginning of the seventeenth century. In other words, the good quarto printed from Shakespeare's manuscript and the bad quarto which derives, at least in part, though by oral transmission only, from the original prompt-book at the Globe, agree in certain readings which are inferior in quality to their F1 variants.

This is rather a serious discovery, and one that appears to threaten our entire critical structure. For either the better readings, "cast", "enurn'd", "rots" and "wisenesse" were found in Shakespeare's original manuscript or they were not. If they were, then not only have we failed so far satisfactorily to probe the textual disorders of Q2 and must continue to search for some further cause of corruption not yet brought to light, but this further cause must be common to both quartos—a contingency which seems very unlikely on the face of it. If, on the other hand, they were not in the original manuscript, then they must have been introduced into the prompt-book after its original preparation and the making-out of players' parts by the bookkeeper, since the agreement of the bad quarto with the good seems to show that they were not heard upon the stage at early performances of the play. This would mean that Shakespeare himself was revising *Hamlet* after these early performances; in other words, we should have to reckon with his interference, as well as that of the slovenly transcriber of 1622, in the F1 text at some date subsequent to the construction of the prompt-copy—a contingency which would throw a disturbing atmosphere of doubt over some of our previous conclusions.

Of one thing at least we can be absolutely clear at the outset; however they got into the F1 text, three of these readings are indubitably Shakespearian in origin.[1]

> And why such daily cast of brazen cannon,

must be the true reading, while "inurn'd" and "wisenesse" are equally authentic. The latter, seen in its context—

> I prithee, take thy fingers from my throat;
> For, though I am not splenitive and rash,
> Yet have I in me something dangerous,
> Which let thy wiseness fear—

gives an edge of irony to Hamlet's threat which "wisdom" lacks, a touch that it would be absurd to credit to Scribe C.

---

[1] The fourth, "rots", is more questionable and will be discussed in vol. II. p. 282.

As for "enurn'd", Shakespeare uses, or misuses, "urn" for "grave" twice elsewhere (*Hen. V*, 1.2.228; *Cor.* 5.6.146), a usage for which the *N.E.D.* quotes no parallel until his imitators came to add it to the resources of their poetic diction. In short, it is inconceivable that a mere copyist can have invented the word.

If these three readings are emendations by Shakespeare of his own text, why not other F1 readings too? Dr W. W. Greg, indeed, is certain that Shakespeare took a hand in the correction of the prompt-book at some date subsequent to its construction. In an appendix to his *Principles of Emendation in Shakespeare* he provides a number of interesting lists of comparative readings from the three main texts of *Hamlet*. The first of these consists of readings in which the bad quarto and F1 agree as against the good quarto, and a sub-section of the list, which is headed "Corrections in the prompt-copy", is prefaced as follows:

There are some readings in Q2 which cannot be regarded as errors of the compositor, but must be supposed to have stood in the autograph, and which are yet so manifestly inferior to those of F1 and Q1 that we can only suppose the latter to have been the author's, or at least authorized, corrections, introduced into the prompt-book previous to the preparation of the actors' parts.[1]

The second list again, which consists of readings in which the two quartos agree as against F1, includes a sub-section entitled "Alterations in the prompt-copy" which opens in similar fashion:

These appear to be deliberate alterations made in the prompt-book while in use, but subsequent to the preparation of the actors' parts. They require to be carefully considered in view of possible authorization by Shakespeare.[2]

The two sub-sections contain twenty-three readings in all,

[1] *Emendation*, p. 56; *Aspects*, p. 183.
[2] *Emendation*, p. 63; *Aspects*, pp. 190–1.

and though Dr Greg does not claim every F1 variant of the twenty-three as Shakespeare's emendation, it is clear from his detailed notes and from the text of his lecture that he considers a fair proportion of them to be so. In other words, his contention is that the "inferior readings" of Q2 are in some cases Shakespeare's first shots for which upon consideration he later substituted his better "second thoughts".

I shall say something about the items in Dr Greg's lists later on; but let us begin by examining his general position. At first sight it appears very strong indeed. That dramatists commonly make alterations and improvements in their plays in the light of rehearsal or performance is common knowledge. That Shakespeare lived in London for about twelve years after *Hamlet* was first seen on the stage in its final form, and was presumably in and about the theatre during the whole of that period, can hardly be denied. The more one considers the external circumstances of the situation the more likely it seems that Shakespeare would have made alterations in *Hamlet* after passing his original manuscript over to his company. And when we find a number of readings in the later (F1) text which are obvious improvements upon their parallels in the earlier (Q2) text it is extremely tempting to invoke the hand of Shakespeare as their source.

And yet, strangely enough, the more one dwells upon the internal facts, the less attractive the theory becomes. If Shakespeare was available in the case of certain readings, why not for very many more? The business is complicated, we must not forget, by the copyist of 1621–2 who introduced bad readings by the score for which the prompt-book was not responsible. But in §§ III and V, we have watched the book-holder at work making out the prompt-copy. We have assigned to him most emendations in F1 for which the presence of a nonsense word in Q2 shows that a word difficult to decipher stood in the original manuscript. And we may assuredly credit him with a fair proportion of those misreadings of Shakespeare's handwriting of which examples have been quoted on p. 150. At times, too, he altered words for no reason except that they seemed obscure or hard to understand. Thus, as we have seen, the changes "scullion" for "stallyon" and "tunes" for "laudes" must have been made in the original prompt-book, since they are both found in Q1. But why trouble to emend or alter, if Shakespeare was there to consult? And if Shakespeare would improve his own "first shots", why did he not also correct the "shots" of the prompter, some of which were very wide of the mark?

What, too, of those other cruxes, to be considered later, in which, as the nonsense in all three texts or in both Q2 and F1 shows, the prompter has clearly been defeated? We moderns, for instance, unconsciously educated by Alexander Dyce, do not wince nor cry aloud when we hear our stage Hamlets talking about a "pajock". But what did Shakespeare make of that strange fowl when he encountered it at rehearsal or performance? Surely, too, he would have found it odd that the actor who played Polonius should say "roaming" instead of "running" (1.3.109), or that Burbadge should utter contradictions in terms like "fond and winnowed opinions".[1] It will be alleged perhaps that Shakespeare's corrections in these instances were made in the players' parts, and that the book-holder did not trouble to introduce them into the prompt-book, which once the play had been committed to memory would be little consulted except for the stage-directions. But this gives no help to Dr Greg, since it explains neither how nonsense words or faulty emendations came to be uttered on the stage as their presence in Q1 proves they were, nor how Shakespeare's "second thoughts" came to be found in the F1 text.

To account for this very striking absence of supervision by Shakespeare in the making of the prompt-book, and

[1] *Vide* vol. II, pp. 328–31.

apparently also in the rehearsing, of his most subtle and elaborate play, is not at first sight easy, though I shall presently suggest a partial explanation; but of the fact itself there can, I think, be little doubt. And this being so, I find it exceedingly difficult to believe in Dr Greg's general thesis of "first shots" in Q2 and "second thoughts" in F1.

Nor does it seem at all impossible, or even troublesome, to assign every one of the readings in Q2 which Dr Greg regards as Shakespeare's first shots (except our four starred variants in the list on p. 149) to one or other of the two agents of corruption whose influence upon that text was the subject of the previous chapter. It is unnecessary to demonstrate this here; Dr Greg's own list is printed in Appendix B with references to pages in this book on which are offered explanations of the various items. As for the three variants still upon our hands, it was Dr Greg himself who first suggested to me the clue to those and a good deal more which is related to them. I pointed out, it will be remembered, that if Shakespeare did not emend his own prompt-book, the only alternative explanation of the variants in question is that they were perpetrated by some corrupting agency we have not yet discovered. This hypothesis seemed, however, difficult to entertain because the agency in question must be shown to have affected both quartos, and both in the same manner, to meet the facts of the situation. Yet there is, as it happens, an easy way round this difficulty. For if we suppose that inferior readings common to the two quartos originated in the bad one, as well they might, and were then transferred to the good one, everything would be explained. And this, as I shall now proceed to show, is precisely what appears to have taken place.

(*b*) Misprints and spellings common to the two quartos and what they tell us

The clue, I say, was first put into my hands by Dr Greg. The earliest of his lists of comparative readings already referred to, the list of readings in which Q1 and F1 agree as against Q2, contains 57 items, in which total, he writes, "the numbers supplied by the several acts are 20, 15, 14, 4, 4; the falling-off being naturally due to the greater divergence of Q1 towards the end of the play".[1] In regard, however, to his second list of readings, viz. those in which Q1 agrees with Q2 as against F1, he has a different story to tell. "Curiously enough," he says, "the number of readings in this group is almost the same as in group (1), namely 55; but the distribution is strikingly different, the numbers in the several acts being 37, 6, 7, 1, 4. The fact that more than two-thirds of the readings come from the first act must, I feel sure, have some important significance for the textual problem, but what this significance can be I am at present unable to imagine."[2] As a matter of fact, my own figures for readings of this class run to 176, over three times as many as Dr Greg's, but as I find 92 of them in the first act my larger total does not affect his argument.[3]

Writing in 1918, I drew attention to a number of bibliographical links between the two quartos in the first act.[4] The links in question were for the most part coincidences in unusual spellings and in misprints, of which the following is a list:

[1] *Emendation*, p. 55; *Aspects*, p. 182.
[2] *Emendation*, p. 60; *Aspects*, p. 187.
[3] *Vide* Appendix A (*a*).
[4] *The Copy for Hamlet, 1603, etc.* pp. 12–15.

Coincident spellings and misprints in the quartos (Act 1)

1.1. 29	approoue	205	gelly
44	*horrowes (Q1 horrors)	1.3. 74	*of a most select (*ditto* F1)
60	Armor (Q1 armor)	1.4. 49	*interr'd
63	smot the sleaded pollax	83	Nemeon Lyons nerue
71	strikt	1.5. 33	rootes...Lethe wharffe
73	*cost		
74	forraine marte	55	Angle (Q1 angle = angel)
75	ship-writes		linckt
169	aduise	64	leaprous
1.2.129	*sallied	67	allies (*ditto* F1)
177	I prethee (Q1 pre thee student	89	Gloworme (Q1 Gloworme)
200	Capapea	151	Sellerige
1.2.204	tronchions		

* *Misprints.*

I attempted at the time to explain these coincidences on the hypothesis that Q1 was partly derived, through an abridged transcript, from an early Shakespearian manuscript of *Hamlet*, which after further revision at length took form as the play printed in Q2. We have learnt a good deal about reported texts since 1918, more especially from Dr Greg's *Alcazar and Orlando*, and I should now hesitate to subscribe to some of my original doctrines about the origin of *Hamlet*, Q1. Yet, there the coincident spellings and misprints are; and taken in conjunction with the ninety-two readings in which the quartos agree as against F1, they prove, I think, beyond dispute, that there was some bibliographical connection between the good and the bad quartos in the first act. A pirate, overhearing a play acted in the theatre, could hardly report spellings and misprints by the score;[1] and moreover, the text he heard was *ex hypothesi*

[1] The couple of coincidences with F1 warn us that he might report misprints if they passed muster on the stage or if he were an actor reproduce spellings he had grown familiar with in his player's part.

the prompt-book version which lies at the back of the F1 *Hamlet*, so that it would seem absurd to saddle him with the responsibility for the ninety-two readings in which the quartos agree to differ from F1. Nevertheless, though the links between the texts of 1603 and 1605 are bibliographical and not oral, unless I am greatly mistaken the source of most of these common spellings, misprints and readings was the reporter and no one else. In other words, they arose not through the influence of Shakespeare's manuscript upon the bad quarto, as I assumed in 1918, but through the influence of the bad quarto upon the good one.

In April 1926, Miss Greta Hjort of Girton College published in the *Modern Language Review* an important article in which she claimed that the printers of the good quarto of *Romeo and Juliet* (1599) made use of the bad quarto (1597) of the same play in the production of their text. The theory, which revives an old suggestion by Gericke in 1879, is discussed and expanded by Dr Greg in another section of his *Principles of Emendation*,[1] and may be taken as proved. Did the printers of *Hamlet*, 1605, in the same way make occasional use of the quarto of 1603? *A priori* there is no reason why they should not have done so. The two editions of *Hamlet* had the same publisher; the 1605 title-page with its advertisement, "Newly imprinted and enlarged to almost as much againe as it was, according to the true and perfect Coppie", suggests that Roberts not only had the earlier text in mind but had actually handled it; and lastly, if the manuscript copy was a difficult one, as we have seen reason for thinking it was, Roberts or his compositor would naturally examine the printed text of 1603 to see if any help was to be got from it. And doing so, he would at first have an encouraging reception, seeing that the bad quarto, as everyone knows, is far closer to the good texts in the opening scenes than elsewhere. The following passages, for instance, differ very slightly indeed in the two quartos: 1.1.59–79

[1] *Emendation*, pp. 49–54; *Aspects*, pp. 175–81.

(21 lines); 1.1.127–75 (=49 lines); 1.2.160–258 (=99 lines); 1.4.38–91 (=54 lines); and the whole of 1.5 (=191 lines). Thus a compositor puzzled by Shakespeare's writing might have found the text of 1603 quite useful for the first act, or rather for the Marcellus scenes of the first act. It would have proved of little service in later acts, and even for the first act he would no doubt have consulted it cautiously, knowing, as he probably did, a good deal about its origin. But I submit that such consultation provides the most satisfactory, if not the only possible, explanation of the phenomena noted above.[1]

And if we examine the coincident misprints in the list just given from act 1, a list which includes "cost" and "interr'd", we shall find that the foregoing hypothesis is not only plausible in itself but eases the interpretation of particular difficulties. It even helps us to think better of the Globe theatre and its ways. I was, for example, for years puzzled by the word "sallied" which is found in both quartos and is, I am convinced, a misprint of "sullied".[2] How came it to be thus misprinted twice? Regard the two quartos as bibliographically independent, and we find ourselves enmeshed in a network of hypothesis including the supposition that the misprint was current on the stage. But allow for the influence of Q1, and all is straightforward. The "sallied" of 1603 becomes merely a misprint of the word "sullied" written by the reporter, which misprint led the compositor of 1605 astray; and "sullied" was the word spoken on the stage from the very first. The same explanation serves for "cost" in 1.1.73 and "rootes" in 1.5.33, while the variant "horrowes"†/"horrors" in 1.1.44 is particularly interesting, because I fancy it gives us a glimpse of the 1605 compositor hesitating between the guidance of the

[1] My impression is that it was consultation only and that it would be going much too far to suppose that act 1 of Q2 was printed from a corrected copy of Q1.

[2] *Vide* vol. II, pp. 307–15 for a lengthy discussion of this reading.

bad quarto and the word which he plainly saw in the copy in front of him.

And what of "interr'd", the second of the variants which started us on this branch of our enquiry? In this case, too, if my hypothesis be sound, "enurn'd" was the word spoken on the stage from the first. It is, however, an unusual word, which a reporter would be unlikely to remember, and for which he would naturally substitute "interr'd" when he came to write up his text. But the unusual word "enurn'd" or "inurn'd" also bothered the compositor in 1605, the more so that in Shakespeare's hand, never clever with minim letters, it would present him with one of the most difficult combination of such letters that can well be imagined. Little wonder if he turned to the printed text of 1603 for help, and finding "interr'd" there, a word not very dissimilar graphically, adopted it without hesitation.

(c) Other "first shots" explained as Q2 misprints

Of our original group of interior readings common to the quartos there remains "wisedome" (wisenesse), which occurs at 5.1.286, far removed from the coincident misprints of act 1, and therefore not to be explained by any theory of printing-house reference to Q1. With it may be grouped two other instances, not yet examined, in which the quartos agree upon a reading which is clearly less authoritative than the F1 parallels. These are:

2.2.43

(F1) Haue I, my Lord? *Assure you*, my good Liege
(Q2) Haue I my Lord? *I assure* my good Liege
(Q1) Haue I my Lord? *I assure* your grace

4.5.188

(F1) Thought, and *Affliction*, Passion, Hell it selfe
(Q2) Thought and *afflictions*, passion, hell it selfe
(Q1) Thoughts & *afflictions*, torments worse than hell

Dr Greg in his list of readings in which the quartos agree as against F1 classes this last among "accidental agreements" in regard to which "it would not be safe...to argue that the reading of Q1 lent any additional support to Q2"; and it is my belief that "wisedome" and "I assure" should be regarded as accidental agreements also. The latter, it will be remembered, was included in my list of seven Q2 miscorrections for the supply of omitted words;[1] and it is easy to see that had the Q2 compositor first set up

> Haue I my Lord? assure my good Liege,

the corrector could not help noticing that a word was missing and would inevitably assume that the word in question was "I". On the other hand, the Q1 reporter, paraphrasing as usual, would be just as likely to write the direct "I assure" as the more formal and poetical "Assure you". Nor, I think, is it placing any strain upon credibility to assume such a coincidence.

In exactly the same way, the substitution of the more ordinary and closely similar word "wisedome" for the unusual "wisenesse" is so natural that it is not in the least difficult to believe it to have been made independently by both the Q1 reporter and the Q2 compositor. It is hardly conceivable, indeed, that the reporter should have avoided such an alteration, while as far as the compositor is concerned, the list of misprints on p. 149 contains two remarkable parallels which it will be illuminating to set forth side by side with the variant we are now considering. Here are the three divergent readings in their contexts:

3.1.160

(F1) Th'expectansie and Rose of the faire State
(Q2) Th'expectation, and Rose of the faire state

4.7.7

(F1) So crimefull, and so Capitall in Nature
(Q2) So criminall and so capitall in nature

---

[1] *Vide* pp. 139–40.

5.1.286

(F1) Which let thy wisenesse feare
(Q2) Which let thy wisedome feare

Dr Greg will, I think, hardly ask us to accept "Th'expecta-tion" as a "first shot" on the part of the dramatist; and yet "criminall" and "wisedome" stand upon exactly the same footing. Viewing the three examples in conjunction, I find it impossible to doubt two things about them: first, that in "expectansie", "crimefull" and "wisenesse" F1 gives us the authentic words of Shakespeare; and second, that their Q2 variants are nothing but vulgarisations on the part of the printer. Indeed, as I have already suggested in regard to "expectansie",[1] the hard-pressed compositor probably caught sight of the first half of the words in Shakespeare's manuscript, and just guessed the rest.[2] At any rate, I can see no reason why any editor of *Hamlet* should lie awake at night bothering his head over the agreement of the quartos in "wisedome"; and I am even prepared to wager that had the reporter of Q1 elected to give us his version of 3.1.160 and 4.7.7, which unhappily he did not, we should have found further agreement in "expectation" and "criminall".

Dr Greg, because he confines his survey to variants in which Q1 is involved, does not include "crimefull" in his list of "corrections in the prompt-copy"; yet "criminall" has as good a claim to be considered a "first shot" of Shakespeare's as any of the other Q2 variants instanced by him, and a good deal better claim than many. Nor is it the only case in point. His self-imposed limits preclude him from mentioning, for example, the variants at 1.5.95, "beare me stiffely vp" (F1), "beare me swiftly vp"(Q2); 2.2.43, "Assure you" (F1), "I assure" (Q2); 3.1.72, "dispriz'd Loue" (F1), "despiz'd loue" (Q2); 3.1.167,

---

[1] *Vide* p. 103.
[2] Cf. 3.2.94: "And scape detecting" (F1),
　　　"And scape detected" (Q2).

"Feature of blowne youth" (F1), "stature of blowne youth" (Q2); 3.3.79, "hyre and Sallery" (F1), "base and silly" (Q2); 3.4.88, "Reason panders Will" (F1), "reason pardons will" (Q2); 4.5.38, "bewept to the graue" (F1), "beweept to the ground" (Q2); 4.5.160, "an old mans life" (F1), "a poore mans life" (Q2); 4.7.20, "Would like the Spring" (F1), "Worke like the spring" (Q2); 4.7.192, "this folly doubts it" (F1), "this folly drownes it" (Q2); 5.1.94, "meant to begge it" (F1), "went to beg it" (Q2); 5.1.252, "haue lodg'd" (F1), "been lodg'd" (Q2); 5.1.260, "sage Requiem" (F1), "a Requiem" (Q2); 5.2.17, "vnseale" (F1), "vnfold" (Q2); 5.2.197, "Beauy" (F1), "breede" (Q2); 5.2.310, "I am affear'd" (F1), "I am sure" (Q2); 5.2.356, "shall liue behind me" (F1), "shall I leaue behind me" (Q2). And yet every one of these seventeen variants is relevant to his argument, and with a little search I have no doubt he might have found as many more again. His lists, in short, are highly selective; and selective lists of this kind are bound to be misleading, because they inevitably suppress a portion of the evidence. Had he, for example, included the seventeen variants just cited, he could hardly, I think, have helped suspecting that misreading on the part of the Q2 compositor might have something to do with them, since, in the case of nine at least, graphical similarity stares one in the face, while further consideration might have shown him that the phenomenon of omission would account for most of the rest.

My own explanation of these readings offers probability, not proof. But Dr Greg's does no more. And probability for probability, which is the more reasonable; that out of a sea of 1300 variants a select handful are to be explained by Shakespearian revision which left the remainder untouched; or that the handful in question are simply part of the general corruption of these texts and to be explained, as I have shown they can be, by the same causes that produced that general corruption?

(d) Shakespeare perhaps abridged the prompt-book

Nevertheless, despite all that has just been said, I think it conceivable that Shakespeare may have handled the prompt-book before (not after) *Hamlet* was put on the stage, and that the F1 text bears traces of his pen. My reasons are not those of Dr Greg, and the evidence is inconclusive and confined to a single scene; but it is evidence I find necessary to state. I should like to evade it, for it would be simpler not to have Shakespeare to reckon with in F1 at all; but though I fought against the possibility for some time, I yielded in the end when I found that Dr Pollard was inclined to take it seriously.

Among the emendations provisionally attributed to Scribe P in § v we encountered, it will be remembered, a particularly successful instance in the following version of 3.4.48–51:

> Heauens face doth glow,
> Yea this solidity and compound masse,
> With tristfull visage as against the doome,
> Is thought-sicke at the act,

which F1 prints in place of Q2's

> heauens face dooes glowe
> Ore this solidity and compound masse
> With heated visage, as against the doome
> Is thought sick at the act.[1]

The obvious seat of the corruption in Q2 is "Ore", which, as I shall later try to show, was probably "and" in Shakespeare's manuscript. In any case, those responsible for the prompt-book must have found the word as difficult to read as the Q2 compositor, since the "Yea" of F1, though restoring what I take to be the original sense, bears no

[1] *Vide* pp. 73–4.

graphical resemblance whatever to "Ore" and is a patent gloss. This gloss I should unhesitatingly attribute to Scribe P, like the other prompt-book emendations referred to above, were it not for the second change in the passage, viz. "tristfull" for "heated", which displays a command of poetic diction too considerable for Scribe C; and though it is probably not beyond Scribe P, one is left asking why a prompter should go out of his way to make this, from his standpoint, quite unnecessary alteration. The probabilities seem to be against it. On the other hand, "heated" is itself far too apt to the context to be attributable to the Q2 corrector. In a word, while I find it hard to believe that "heated" can have come from any other pen than Shakespeare's, "tristfull" may well have done so likewise.

And there is a further point about the passage. It belongs to 3.4, the scene, it will be recalled, in which when reviewing the indications of playhouse abridgment in F1 we discovered cuts of a kind so skilful and considerate, that as I put it in § III, "Shakespeare himself could hardly have pruned his own verse more tenderly", while Dr Pollard, reading through the proofs of this book, and confronted with the two passages quoted on pp. 28–9, wrote in the margin "I should like to believe that Shakespeare did this pruning himself". Now these two impressions, shared by Dr Pollard and myself, that Shakespeare may be (i) behind the cuts in 3.4.71–81 and 161–70, and (ii) also behind the verbal changes in 3.4.48–51, are impressions only. But they were arrived at while weighing the points independently, and I think it is fair to say that they lend each other a certain amount of mutual support. Nor is it at all difficult to frame a hypothesis, consonant with the general probabilities of the situation, which would at once explain Shakespeare's handling of the prompt-book in this scene, and render that handling more likely. If we suppose, to begin with, that the first stage in the making of the prompt-book of 1601 was the transcription of the whole text, apart from the stage-directions, by some copyist at the Globe in preparation for action by the prompter, the copyist would inevitably have drawn attention to the inordinate length of the play, and the prompter might well have laid the completed transcript before Shakespeare with an intimation that it must be cut down by at least 200 lines, especially in Burbadge's part,[1] if anything further was to be done with it. On this theory, surely not at all an incredible one, Shakespeare would have been a reluctant agent for most of the abridgment in the F1 text, and would himself have been immediately, though not of course morally, responsible for that blunting of his finer dramatic points which the cuts in Act 1, for example, effected.[2]

There would, of course, be no need for him to read through the whole prompt-book for the purpose of the operation; he knew well enough where to look for material best suited to the knife. Osric and the lord who follows him would be obvious victims, and he would soon realise with chagrin that to throw the fourth soliloquy and its context overboard might save fifty-seven lines, mostly Burbadge's! A little too could be cut away here and there from 3.4 and 4.7. And as he read the former scene through, his eye would naturally catch lines in which, owing to his difficult handwriting, words had probably been misread by the Globe transcriber, as they were later by the Q2 compositor, so that it is perhaps no accident that two of the Q2 cruxes (cf. ll. 162, 169) occur in passages deleted in F1. On the other hand, ll. 48–51, just quoted, form a digression inviting excision, and would probably have received it, had not the final word "act" been awkwardly involved with the Queen's speech that follows. We can imagine Shakespeare hovering over it with uplifted pen for a moment in doubt, sparing it to pass on to a cut twenty lines later, but before doing so altering to "Yea" some nonsense word which

[1] *Vide* p. 24.
[2] *Vide* p. 25.

stood at the beginning of l. 49, and, finding "heated" in the next line no longer to his taste, writing in "tristfull" instead.

If this fancy picture be anything like the truth, it is arguable that restorations and improvements by Shakespeare may be looked for in other scenes containing cuts. In view of the general condition of the prompt-book, however, we ought, I think, to be very chary of pressing such possibilities to any length. It is noteworthy, in particular, that a bad crux stands in both texts in the line immediately before the F1 cuts at 5.2.204–18, so that there at any rate Shakespeare had not looked at the context. Or take the interesting variants at 3.3.5–7, already quoted in Chapter 1:

Q2

The termes of our estate may not endure
Hazerd so neer's as doth hourely grow
Out of his browes

F1

The terms of our estate, may not endure
Hazard so dangerous as doth hourely grow
Out of his Lunacies.

Here the similarity with the variants at 3.4.48–51 is at first sight so striking that we are strongly tempted to assign the double change to the same cause. And yet, when we examine the readings more narrowly, it must be admitted that, though there is nothing wrong with "Lunacies" as regards sense or metre, "dangerous" does not really better "neer's", as "tristfull" might seem to better "heated". On the contrary "hazard so dangerous" is, as I have noted above,[1] tautological, and altogether weaker than "hazerd so neer's", which conveys at once royal dignity and a sense of personal menace. In other words, the substitution is just the kind of inattentive alteration that we expect from Scribe C; I do not doubt that he is responsible for it, and

[1] *Vide* p. 9.

this being so, I have no difficulty in ascribing to the prompter the emendation "Lunacies", the meaning required being obvious from the context.

The mystery of Shakespeare's lack of interest in the prompt-book and also, it would seem, in the rehearsal and performance of the play, is in no way touched by an admission that he may have taken a hand in the abridgment and made a small alteration here and there, while it is assuredly safer to set down all F1 changes to one or other of the two playhouse agents unless we have very good reason to suspect Shakespeare himself. And I can find no good reasons except in 3.4, and no reason at all for his interference with the prompt-book, once rehearsals had begun.

§IX. AUTHOR AND PRODUCER

Setting aside, then, the theory of later interference by Shakespeare, our account of the history of the authoritative *Hamlet* from the day, sometime probably in the late summer of 1601, when a rather untidy manuscript was handed over at the Globe, to the publication of F1 in 1623, is now clear and straightforward. Three separate lines of textual development were laid down in that period, two closely connected together and the third entirely independent. First there was the prompt-book, copied it is true from the autograph original, but furnished with fresh stage-directions and adapted by the bookkeeper for the purposes of performance, a process which included emendation, apparently without reference to the author beyond an instruction that it should be abridged. What happened eventually to this prompt-book is not known, though it would be worth enquiring whether there is any evidence of its being consulted for the editing of F2 in 1632,[1] or for the "Players' Quartos" of 1676. We may assume, at any rate, it or a

---

[1] *Vide* an article by Professor Allardyce Nicoll in *Studies in the First Folio* (Shak. Assoc.), pp. 163–6.

transcript of it was used for performances of *Hamlet* up to the end of Shakespeare's life, and it was certainly in existence in 1621 or 1622, when it was copied in its turn by a playhouse scrivener belonging to the Globe staff to supply Jaggard with a text of *Hamlet* for F1. With this transcription and its publication in the Folio of 1623 begins the second line of textual development, a development still active, too active, to-day.

For the inauguration of the third line we have to go back to Shakespeare's original manuscript of 1601, which after serving at the Globe for the preparation of the prompt-book was of no further use to the company, and found its way into the hands of James Roberts, who was probably commissioned to print it as rejoinder to the publication of the pirated *Hamlet* of 1603. In any event, it was being printed at the end of the following year and was published early in 1605, thus furnishing the modern world with an alternative to the F1 text, and one, as is now I hope abundantly evident, of far greater authority.

Yet it is no absolute alternative. Of the two "ancient copies" Q2 is indisputably "entitled to preference", but it cannot possibly be edited without the aid of the F1 text. From F1 alone can be supplied those twenty-nine lines or half-lines, those ninety-six words and phrases and those five long passages which are lacking in Q2. Further than this, though it is now clear that we must desert all tradition by taking the text of 1605 instead of the text of 1623 as the basis of our own, it is equally clear that we shall be obliged to consult the dethroned text at every step of our journey. And such consultation, if it is to have any value whatever, must be inspired with a confident knowledge of the composition and provenance of both texts. It has been the purpose of sections III–VIII of this book to attain that knowledge; and though the path has been long, and I fear often not a little tedious, it has led us to the goal, or so at least I venture to hope. For we know where we stand. We

know that in the F1 *Hamlet* we have to do with two successive transcribers, and can distinguish their characteristics
sufficiently to be able to assign any particular reading with
fair probability to one or the other. We are confident also
that Q2 was printed from Shakespeare's autograph, and
though it is a sorry piece of printing, we know the causes
of its defects and are, once again, in a position to offer a
plausible explanation of every misprint in the text. These
findings constitute the critical apparatus for the editing of
Hamlet, an apparatus we must now put to use.

But they have also a wider reference than that of textual
problems in *Hamlet*. If they are sound, they provide new
and important information (it is true only of an inferential
character) concerning the relations between Shakespeare
and his company. All we know about those relations hitherto
is that Shakespeare was a sharer in the company, ranking as
one of the principal men, that he acted with them at least
occasionally (he is mentioned in the list of actors prefixed
to Jonson's *Sejanus*, 1603), and that he was their chief
writer. Sir Edmund Chambers suggests that he discon-
tinued regular acting at a fairly early date in his career, and
that "his plays, together, perhaps, with the oversight of
their production, were accepted as a sufficient return for
his share in the company".[1] It is just in regard to this
matter of oversight that the evidence of the *Hamlet* texts
appears most illuminating. For the only conclusion to be
drawn from it is that, at any rate in the production of
Hamlet itself, Shakespeare exercised no supervision of any
kind. On the contrary, we have seen his stage-directions
altered or ignored, his text freely emended and his punctuation revised from beginning to end; while if, as is possible,
he carried through most of the abridgment himself he did
so at the dictation of someone else. It looks as if once the
manuscript had been handed in at the Globe, his control
over it ceased. The presiding genius of theatrical production,

[1] *William Shakespeare*, I, 84.

whoever he may have been, did not even trouble to consult the author when he could not decipher a word or understand a passage.

This suggests either Shakespeare's absence from London at the time *Hamlet* was being produced or a complete separation of function between the playwright and the producer, a separation which we should expect in the case of "literary" dramatists like Greene or Nashe, Beaumont and Fletcher, but which is surprising in a sharer like Shakespeare. And yet if such a separation were traditional, is it not conceivable that the producer of the Chamberlain-King's men was a stickler for rights within his own territory? He probably thought he knew what belonged to a play, or at any rate to performance, as much as Will Shakespeare did, who was after all according to hearsay no "extraordinary" actor. Indeed, in his own conceit, such a producer may have known better; for was not Shakespeare displaying a growing fondness for out-of-the-way words, words which would be "caviary to the general"—a fault one must be on the look-out to amend? Thus he alters "comart" to "cou'nant", "stallion" to "scullion", "prescripts" to "precepts", "lauds" to "tunes", "crants" to "rites" and so on. The F1 *Hamlet*, even when every allowance has been made for the iniquities of Scribe C, is a proof that the company and its principal dramatist did not see eye to eye and that the company's views were final.

Not that Shakespeare's case went unheard. No other play is so full of references to the theatre or of personal expressions of opinion on theatrical technique; for few will dispute that when Hamlet speaks about acting he is his creator's mouthpiece. Probably the Aeneas speech, the mention of players that "have so strutted and bellowed", and the condemnation of clowns who "speak more than is set down for them" had some point for Alleyn's company or rivals of another playhouse; but it would be like Shakespeare to cast oblique glances at his own fellows at the same

time. Is he not talking, indeed, directly at them in his
advice to the player upon stage-elocution? And if we
accept the light punctuation of Q2 as a representation in
print of that pronunciation "trippingly on the tongue"
which the Prince of Denmark commends, what are we to
make of the heavy rhetorical punctuation of F1? Did the
players, those "robustious periwig-pated fellows", insist
upon mouthing their speeches and tearing their passion to
tatters? Is the contrast between the two texts a relic of a
battle of the colons at the Globe?[1] We ask and ask, and
a definite answer will never, can never, be granted to our
questions. But one thing at least we may venture to suspect
that (always assuming Shakespeare to have been in London)
Hamlet was not merely a turning-point in his career
dramatically, but also marked some kind of crisis in his relations with his company. Finally, there is another point,
arising out of our investigations, which is perhaps worth
making. Mr W. J. Lawrence recently characterised the
"full-length *Hamlet*", that is to say the text which contains
the passages omitted from either Q2 or F1, as "a mon-
strosity, the creation of scholarly compromise". We have
seen that, on the contrary, such a text must represent the
Hamlet which Shakespeare himself handed over to the
players in 1601. Whether he imagined that they would
perform a play of over 3760 lines without abridgment we
do not know. If he did he discovered his mistake; but
when we play or print it in full we assuredly need not
hesitate to assume his authority for so doing.[2]

[1] *Vide* vol. II, pp. 194–6.
[2] On the question of the length of Elizabethan plays in general
and of Shakespeare's in particular, *vide* interesting articles by Mr
Alfred Hart in *The Review of English Studies*, 1932, 1934.